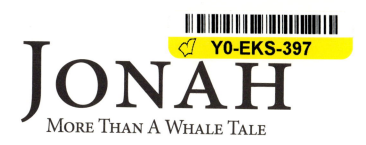

JONAH

MORE THAN A WHALE TALE

BY

JEFF W. JOHNSON

PUBLISHED BY CALVARY DOWNEY PUBLISHING

DOWNEY, CA

2011

JONAH: MORE THAN A WHALE TALE

Copyright © 2011 by Mark Maciel, Calvary Downey Publishing

Published by Calvary Downey Publishing
12808 Woodruff Ave, Downey, CA 90242

First printing, 2011

Unless otherwise noted, all Scripture quotations are taken from the King James Version.

Library of Congress Control number: 2011925325

ISBN: 0-9668433-3-9

Printed in the United States of America.

Editor: Sarah MacNaughton

Cover design: Davey Armstrong

Special thanks to Robbie Boyd, Geri Jones, Hector and Florence Placencia, and Lisa Lewis for their significant contributions to this work.

FOREWORD

Jonah's first chapter shows the frustration that people will experience when they think that they can run away from God or hide from His call upon their lives. Someone once said that a wise man will learn from the mistakes of others. The book of Jonah is a classic example of the problems a man can create for himself when he is foolish enough to think that he can run away from the Almighty God.

As David noted in Psalm 139:

> *Whither shall I go from Thy spirit? or whither shall I flee from Thy presence? If I ascend up into heaven, Thou art there: if I make my bed in hell, behold, Thou art there. If I take the wings of the morning, and dwell in the uttermost parts of the sea; Even there shall Thy hand lead me, and Thy right hand shall hold me.*

In this easy-to-read and instructive study, Pastor Jeff provides excellent insights into the story of Jonah, proving that it is indeed MORE THAN A WHALE TALE.

In Him,

Pastor Chuck Smith
Calvary Chapel Costa Mesa

ILLUSTRATIONS

TABLE OF CONTENTS

Prologue

Have you ever felt a reluctance to do God's will or go God's way? Have you ever intentionally run from God's commands? Like Jonah, many of us have wrestled with following God's call, and we can identify with Jonah's story. Within each one of us is that unwilling prophet, reluctant to do God's bidding. We find a striking similarity between Jonah and the prodigal son in the New Testament. You could almost call Jonah the Old Testament's prodigal son! Jonah stubbornly resists God's call, but as He did with the prodigal son, God calls Jonah back to Himself.

When I think about the book of Jonah, I cannot help but reflect on **Romans 12:1-2**. The apostle Paul writes:

> *I beseech you therefore, brethren, by the mercies of God, that ye present your bodies a living sacrifice, holy, acceptable unto God, which is your reasonable service. And be not conformed to this world: but be ye transformed by the renewing of your mind, that ye may prove what is that good, and acceptable, and perfect, will of God.*

After all Christ has done for us—forgiving our sins, washing away our shame and guilt, and making us right before Him—the most reasonable thing we can do is to give Him our lives saying, "Lord, here I am. Send me."

As we read through Jonah, we see that this minor prophet talks about some major topics! In one respect, this book is unlike the other Minor Prophets. Jonah is the exception in that he only delivers one real prophecy.

And Jonah began to enter into the city a day's journey, and he cried, and said, Yet forty days, and Nineveh shall be overthrown.

Jonah 3:4

In the final eight words of this verse, Jonah both prophesies and preaches. Jonah forth-tells, not fore-tells, God's Word. What I mean by forth-telling is that rather than merely predicting future events, Jonah shares the Gospel in such a way that it penetrates the hearts of those who hear it. For generations, God has used the book of Jonah to minister to hard hearts. Jonah is such an important book that the Jews read it on Yom Kippur. No matter where you are in life, this book will touch your heart and cause you to identify with Jonah.

In Jonah, each of the four chapters represents a different issue, followed by God's response to that issue. Also, every chapter shows us key elements of God's character. Jonah is brought forth in two acts, much like a play.

Four Issues in Two Acts

- Act I: Chapters 1 and 2

- Act II: Chapters 3 and 4

Act I: The Great Sea

Chapter One: Running Away From God

Think for a moment of the prodigal son in **Luke 15**. He ran away from home, squandered his inheritance, and ended up feeding alongside pigs. Because of his foolishness, he literally had nothing. In the same way, Jonah resisted and ended up in the belly of a fish before finally obeying God's command to go to Nineveh. Both of these men resisted God's call, but God reveals His patience by waiting for them to return to Him.

Chapter Two: Running Back to God

When the prodigal son reaches the breaking point, he finally returns home. Like a movie in slow motion, I can picture his homecoming scene: as he walks up the road towards his father's house, his father sees him and runs to greet his lost son with open arms. The father in this parable stands for God the Father, and the prodigal son represents us. We strive to get away from God before we finally hit the wall saying, "I don't care how I serve the Lord. I just want to be right with Him." Like the prodigal son, Jonah tries to escape from God, but he realizes his sin and asks for forgiveness and deliverance. The second chapter reveals God's pardon in response to Jonah's prayer.

Act II: The Great City

Chapter Three: Running With God

Chapter three begins the second act of Jonah as he finally heeds God's command and goes to Nineveh. Here, God reveals His power through Jonah's preaching to the Ninevites.

Chapter Four: Running Ahead of God

The final chapter of this book reveals God's pity even though Jonah pouts and disagrees with Him.

As we study Jonah, God will work in our hearts. He wants to plant His Word within us so that we grow and bring forth fruit in our lives. Occasionally we bog down, only experiencing little spurts of spiritual blessing. Sometimes our well runs dry and we find ourselves spiritually barren! The life-changing truths found in the four chapters of Jonah will break up the logjams in our lives. You see, God wants His Spirit to run freely from within us, overflowing to bless others. **John 7:37-38** says:

> *In the last day, that great day of the feast, Jesus stood and cried, saying, If any man thirst, let him come unto me, and drink. He that believeth on me, as the scripture hath said, out of his belly shall flow rivers of living water.*

The History of Jonah

Jonah prophesied during Jeroboam II's peaceful reign over Israel. However, by the eighth century B.C., Israel had passed from prosperity to judgment and experienced much spiritual darkness and confusion. It is during this time-period that we see the book of Jonah emerge.

In order to fully understand what we are studying, let's take a look at Jonah's origins. First, we must realize that Jonah is neither a story of antiquity nor is it mythology. Some individuals interpret Jonah as an allegory. They take all the elements of the story and make them symbolize something else. For example, Jonah might represent the Jews, or the sea might stand for all the nations of Israel. The fundamental problem here is that an allegory is not a literal event, but this book is! Jonah is historically and literally true, and we have so much to learn from this amazing book. We first see Jonah mentioned during the reign of King Jeroboam II.[i] **II Kings 14:25** states,

---

i Jonah was a contemporary of Hosea and Amos, two other minor prophets. This would most likely put Ashur-Dan III as king of Assyria at the time of Jonah's visit to Nineveh.

> *He restored the coast of Israel from the*
> *entering of Hamath unto the sea of the plain,*
> *according to the word of the Lord God of*
> *Israel, which he spake by the hand of his*
> *servant Jonah, the son of Amittai, the prophet,*
> *which was of Gathhepher.*

Gathhepher, an area near Nazareth in the northern part of Israel, is in the region of Galilee. This is significant, because an interesting exchange took place many years later concerning prophets from Galilee. In **John 7:52,** Jesus speaks with some of the religious rulers, and they question His identity:

> *"They answered and said unto him, Art thou*
> *also of Galilee? Search, and look: for out of*
> *Galilee ariseth no prophet."*

These religious men were not as studious as they pretended! In addition to Jonah, the prophet Nahum was also from Galilee. Jesus took these rulers to task for their lack of knowledge. They missed the blessing of truly knowing God's Word. Jonah also came from the same region as Jesus, who makes several parallels throughout scripture between Himself and Jonah.

Jesus acknowledges Jonah throughout Scripture, proving conclusively that Jonah was a real, historical person. In fact, Jesus identifies Himself with Jonah. For example, **Matthew 12:38-40** records this exchange:

> *Then certain of the scribes and of the*
> *Pharisees answered, saying, Master, we*
> *would see a sign from thee. But he answered*
> *and said unto them, An evil and adulterous*
> *generation seeketh after a sign; and there*
> *shall no sign be given to it, but the sign of the*

> *prophet Jonah: For as Jonah was three days*
> *and three nights in the whale's belly; so shall*
> *the Son of Man be three days and three nights*
> *in the heart of the earth.*

Again, in **Luke 11:30**, Jesus puts His seal of approval on Jonah:

> *"For as Jonas was a sign unto the Ninevites,*
> *so shall also the Son of Man be to this*
> *generation."*

With all the evidence that Jesus gives regarding Jonah, we often wonder why people still criticize this book and refuse to take it literally. Often, the individuals who mock certain biblical teachings have not taken the time to study the scriptures for themselves. Jesus, knowing that His words would come under attack, left ample evidence for us throughout scripture.

Now that we have seen an overview of Jonah's contents and background, let us delve into this amazing book and discover the joys and truth that God has in store for us.

CHAPTER 1

RUNNING AWAY FROM GOD

*"Now the word of the LORD came unto Jonah
the son of Amittai, saying."*   **Jonah 1:1**

How did God speak to the prophets? This first verse shows us that the *"word of the Lord came unto Jonah."* We see the phrase "the word of the Lord came" mentioned in many of the prophetic books, including Hosea, Joel, and Micah. The Lord clearly and unmistakably spoke to His prophets. However, Jonah was the only prophet recorded to actually run away from the Lord.

"Arise, go to Nineveh, that great city, and cry against it; for their wickedness is come up before me."   **Jonah 1:2**

God now commissions Jonah to go to the Gentiles in the Assyrian city of Nineveh.[i] Located on the east side of the Tigress River, far north of Israel, Nineveh was the greatest city of its time. Estimates say that the city walls contained 1,500 towers, each one around 250 feet high. The walls themselves were 100 feet high, 40 feet wide, and surrounded the city in a 60-mile radius. You could drive three chariots side by side on top of them! Not only was Nineveh huge, it was also a stunning city to behold. There were hanging gardens, and

---

i Nineveh is first mentioned in the Bible in Genesis 10:11 as being founded by Nimrod. The entire book of Nahum is a prophetic judgment specifically against the city of Nineveh. Many Assyrian kings had palaces in Nineveh throughout the history of the Assyrian Empire, until it reached its peak during the reign of Sennacherib in 705 B.C.

sparkling gates of gold and ivory. If you walked through it, you would see palaces, temples, and marble courts. It was home to around 600,000 inhabitants.

In contrast to Nineveh's beautiful exterior, its society had horrific practices. First, like many pagan nations, they used slave labor to build their city. Some scholars compare the Ninevites to the Nazis because of the tortures both groups inflicted on their captives. The Ninevites came up with horrendous ways to kill their prisoners. They would gouge out their eyes, cut off their tongues, and lead them around naked, placing hooks through their mouths to keep them in line. They would even skin the men alive and impale them on a pole, leaving them to die slowly.

Surrounding nations greatly feared the Assyrians because of their strength and cruelty. When the Assyrian armies invaded a city they would level it, burning everything from buildings to trees. Many believed it would be better to commit suicide than allow the Assyrians to capture them.[ii]

Can you imagine God saying to you, "Guess what? I am calling you to Berlin. You will be my witness to Germany, the Nazis, and even Hitler himself." That is the kind of calling Jonah received!

But Jonah rose up to flee unto Tarshish from
the presence of the LORD, and went down to

---

ii The Assyrian Empire dates back to the 18th century B.C., and was considered a major power in the ancient near east region from roughly 900 B.C. to 612 B.C. Its borders fluctuated during these three centuries, often reaching Israel and even as far as Egypt. Many encounters between Israel and Assyria are recorded in the books of I and II Kings, Chronicles, and the Prophets. The heart of the empire was located in what is modern day northern Iraq.

FIG. 1

Adad
Gate

Nergal
Gate

Mashki
Gate

Kuyunjik

River Khosr

Shamash
Gate

Nebi
Yunus

Halzi
Gate

Nineveh
City Wall & Gates

0   1km

> *Joppa; and he found a ship going to Tarshish: so he paid the fare thereof, and went down into it, to go with them unto Tarshish from the presence of the LORD.*   **Jonah 1:3**

We can understand Jonah's reluctance to heed God's difficult request, but his response was sinful. Instead of trusting his life to God's care, he ran away. An old expression says, "It is in obedience that we find strength." The Gospel of John shows us a wonderful illustration of this truth. In John chapter four, we find Jesus talking to the Samaritan woman while the disciples have gone shopping for food. As Jesus witnessed to this woman, she realized that He was the Messiah! Excited, she ran to tell the whole village.

When Jesus' disciples returned, they offered Him food, but he refused it. They began questioning, "Who gave the Master something to eat?" But Jesus said, "My meat is to do the will of Him that sent Me, and to finish His work." To Jesus, obeying the Father's will was sustenance enough. Jesus Himself is our example here. His satisfaction and fulfillment came from obedience to the Father, just as ours should.

To Jonah, on the other hand, God's will was like bitter medicine. He did not want to obey, so he fled. Jonah's response was a human one. Perhaps he felt that God was asking just a little too much of him. He knew how the Ninevites treated their enemies, and he was scared of them! This is a tremendous lesson for believers today. You see, Jonah got away from the real issue, which was doing the will of the Father.

Jonah not only disobeyed, but he also had another problem. He refused to love his enemies. God sent Jonah to the

Ninevites out of love, but Jonah certainly did not reciprocate. We see the root of that problem in **Jonah 4:2**. Jonah says,

> *"I knew that thou art a gracious God, and merciful, slow to anger, and of great kindness, and repentest thee of the evil."*

Jonah knew that God was gracious, loving, and full of mercy, and this bothered him. Frankly, he wanted to see the Ninevites perish without salvation. In **Luke 6:46**, Jesus said,

> *"And why call ye me, Lord, Lord, and do not the things which I say?"*

Why do we profess our love for the Lord and still disobey Him? We may lift our hands to heaven, promising to follow Him. We may give of our time and our money. Perhaps we serve in ministry and go to church every Sunday and every Wednesday. Yet all our lip service is in vain if we do not obey Him. God wants to reach the deepest issues in our lives. He does not desire sacrifice; He desires obedience. That is the bottom line.

Jonah had two choices: either go to Nineveh, which was obedience, or go to Tarshish, which was rebellion.[iii] Remember that Jonah was a prophet. He knew God's Word. I wonder if he remembered **Psalm 139:7-10**:

> *Whither shall I go from thy spirit? Or whither*

---

iii Tarshish was a city located in southern Spain and was the furthest western port that the Phoenician sailors would travel. It was located over 2,000 miles west of Joppa and illustrates the extent of Jonah's rebellion. Instead of traveling 500 miles east across the desert to Nineveh, Jonah was attempting to travel to the farthest possible destination by sea in the opposite direction.

shall I flee from thy presence? If I ascend up into heaven, thou art there: if I make my bed in hell, behold, thou art there. If I take the wings of the morning, and dwell in the uttermost parts of the sea; Even there shall thy hand lead me, and thy right hand shall hold me.

Where did Jonah think he could run? I remember years ago, when a friend called to tell me that he had found God in Hawaii. I was not a Christian at the time, yet I was searching everywhere for God. I said, "You mean I can just go to Hawaii and God will be there?" My friend said, "Yeah!" Obviously I could not find God in Los Angeles. I thought all I had to do was go to Hawaii to find Him.

We cannot run from the presence of the Lord. God is in Los Angeles. God is in Hawaii. God is everywhere! Jonah became so wrapped up in not doing the will of the Lord that he deceived himself into thinking he could hide from an omnipresent God.

When God gives gifts to His people, they sometimes come with responsibilities. He promises to care for us, but He does not promise that His way will be easy. God called Jonah to prophesy, but Jonah felt like giving up before he even started! Other men whom God called had similar experiences: Moses, Elijah, and Jeremiah all felt like giving up at some point. We can relate to this. Struggles and frustrations arise, and we just want to throw in the towel and say, "Forget it! I can't do this!" However, these men of God set an example of perseverance. God places struggles in our path to help us grow. You see, Jonah needed Nineveh as much as Nineveh needed Jonah.

As we faithfully accomplish God's will, we grow in grace, slowly changing into the image of Christ. Think of the circumstances in your spiritual life. Do you find yourself making excuses to skip church or to forego your nightly devotions? In times like these, choose Christ. The Lord promises to meet you there and bless you for seeking Him. This does not mean that our struggles will diminish, but we will receive strength from God to make wise decisions when our flesh tries to rebel against the Spirit.

Hebrews 4:12 reminds us of the power of Scripture:

> *The word of God is quick, and powerful, and sharper than any two edged sword, piercing even to the dividing asunder of soul and spirit, and of the joints and marrow, and is a discerner of the thoughts and intents of the heart.*

Jonah did not comprehend the severity of his circumstances. He thought things were working in his favor! As he ran to the docks at Joppa, Jonah saw his plan coming together, not falling apart. No doubt he thought his escape would be successful! It is just like the enemy to deceive God's peoples this way. Satan will always have a ship ready and waiting for you. He will always say, "Run for it! I've made things easy for you!" Every time the enemy tries to deceive, things will flow without a hitch. Satan wants us to believe that we are doing the right thing, but all the while he is drawing us away from God as fast as he can.

Jonah's situation worsened as he ran westward to Joppa.[iv]

---

iv Joppa, meaning beauty, was a town in the territory given to the tribe of Dan. In Joshua 19:46 it is called "Japho". It is located between Caesarea and Gaza, at a distance of 30 miles

Interestingly, he fled in the complete opposite direction of Nineveh, which lies to the east. Joppa was a port city located just south of modern day Tel Aviv, right on the coast of the Mediterranean Sea. At one time, Joppa was a gigantic port for Phoenician[v] ships that took people and supplies all around the world. Jonah ran to Joppa to avoid witnessing to the Gentiles. Years later, an interesting parallel occurred in Joppa. While the apostle Peter was staying there, God commanded him to witness to the Gentiles; but unlike Jonah, Peter obeyed.

The scripture literally says: "Jonah went *down* to Joppa." As soon as he decided to disobey, Jonah was headed downward! He continued his descent into the ship and eventually deep into the sea. Any time we go our way instead of God's way, we head downward.[vi] Jonah paid his fare to get on the ship, but he also paid the price for his rebellion. Sin is expensive and not just monetarily! Disobedience always makes us spiral downward, and we pay for our sins over and over again.

---

northwest from Jerusalem. Joppa is believed to be one of the oldest cities in the world. It was the chief seaport of Judea, although it remained under the control of the Phoenicians. The materials for both the first and second temples were landed in Joppa (2 Chr. 2:16, Ezra 3:7). In Acts chapter nine, Peter resides at Simon the tanner's house, which is in Joppa. Here, Paul received the vision of the sheet and the subsequent call to preach the gospel to the Gentiles (Acts 9:36–43).

v "The Phoenicians were renowned in ancient times for the manufacturing of glass, and some of the specimens of this work that have been preserved are still the wonder of mankind … In the matter of shipping, whether ship-building be thought of or traffic upon the sea, the Phoenicians surpassed all other nations." Easton, M.G. Easton's Bible Dictionary. Oak Harbor, WA: Logos Research Systems, Inc., 1996.

vi The words "went down" record Jonah's descent into disobedience.
Chapter 1:3 – He went down to Joppa.
Chapter 1:3 – He went down into the ship.
Chapter 1:5 – He went down to the inner part of the ship.
Chapter 2:6 – He went down into the fish and the deepest parts of the sea.

> *"But the LORD sent out a great wind into the sea, and there was a mighty tempest in the sea, so that the ship was like to be broken."*
>
> **Jonah 1:4**

Though Jonah thought his escape plan was working, he ended up right where God wanted him. In verse four, God begins the active process of rebuking Jonah by stirring up the wind and the sea. It is a fearful thing to fall into the hands of an angry God, yet Jonah has done just that.

Also in verse four, we see God's first miracle in the book of Jonah. He sends a storm. **Psalm 107:23-29** perfectly illustrates what happened to Jonah:

> *They that go down to the sea in ships, that do business in great waters; these see the works of the LORD, and his wonders in the deep. For He commandeth, and raiseth the stormy wind, which lifteth up the waves thereof. They mount up to the heaven, they go down again to the depths: their soul is melted because of trouble. They reel to and fro, and stagger like a drunken man, and are at their wits' end. Then they cry unto the LORD in their trouble, and he bringeth them out of their distresses. He maketh the storm a calm, so that the waves thereof are still.*

God uses storms to wake us up. He wants our attention because He loves us. Granted, not all storms occur because of sin. When the disciples encountered the storm on the Sea

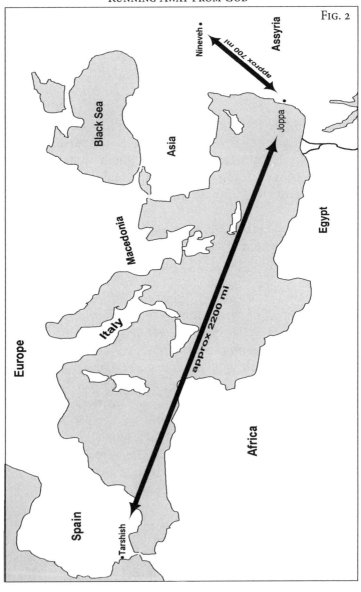

FIG. 2

of Galilee, it was not because of sin. In that situation, God caused the storm in order to build up their faith. He wanted them to trust and obey Him and to see what an awesome God they served. Keep in mind that Jesus was in the boat with the disciples when the storm sprang up.

We find some interesting similarities between Jonah's storm and the storm that Jesus and His disciples weathered on Galilee. First, both Jonah and Jesus slept soundly while the storm raged. Next, Jonah's crewman and Jesus' disciples feared for their lives. In both cases, the crews woke up the sleeping men. Perhaps most fascinating is that in both cases the storms stopped once the sleeping men awoke. In Jonah's case, he was thrown overboard and the storm ceased. Jesus simply quieted the storm through His own power. Both of these events caused the men on board to greatly fear the Lord.

Jonah was called to be a blessing in the same way that God called the Jews to be a blessing in **Genesis 12:2.**

> *"And I will make of thee a great nation, and I will bless thee, and make thy name great; and thou shalt be a blessing."*

When he rebelled, Jonah was the opposite of a blessing; instead, he caused trouble for everyone around him. We find other examples of this happening in the Scripture. For instance, Abraham lied about his wife in **Genesis 12**. Fear caused him to mislead Pharaoh, who nearly took Sarah for his harem. When Pharaoh discovered Abraham's lie, he sternly rebuked him. Like Jonah, Abraham brought more trouble than blessings.

Our sin hurts everyone we come in contact with. Like a wave pounding against a rock, our wrongdoing often has continuing negative effects. Many times, we hurt people we don't even know! Here, Jonah loses the voice of God, falls deep in sin, and places those around him in harm's way. Jonah experienced these troubles simply because he failed to obey God and, instead, ran as far and as fast as he could:

> *Then the mariners were afraid, and cried every man unto his god, and cast forth the wares that were in the ship into the sea, to lighten it of them. But Jonah was gone down into the sides of the ship; and he lay, and was fast asleep.*
> **Jonah 1:5**

Verse five tells us that the mariners were afraid. Think, for a moment, what that means. These men were salty sailors from Phoenicia! They were tough hands and had sailed the proverbial seven seas. They knew everything there was to know about sailing and had surely faced fierce storms before. Yet this particular storm makes them fear for their lives and cry out to their gods. The sailors' reactions tip us off as to how serious this situation truly is.

Jonah's storm reminds me of a similar story: a female passenger aboard a ship stands on deck with the captain. The ship is surrounded by thick fog. They hear a foghorn in the distance but cannot even see beyond the ship's railing. They know another ship is near, but they cannot see it and fear a collision. The captain turns to the woman and says, "Well, we have done all that we can do."

The woman says, "Isn't there anything else we can do to get out of this fog?"

The captain replies, "Yes. We can pray."
She responds, "Is it that bad?"

Many times we pray as a last resort. The mariners on the
boat with Jonah realize they have no other choice and begin
praying to their own gods.

In addition to praying, the mariners also start throwing
things overboard in hopes of keeping the ship afloat and
gaining better control. Meanwhile, Jonah goes down into
the ship and sleeps soundly despite the raging storm. While
the Phoenician mariners are terrified, Jonah snores away.
You may ask, "How can he sleep through such commotion?"
Jonah slept because he was running away from God. Through
sleep, Jonah escaped from reality. Satan fooled him again.
Jonah lost his spiritual health and energy, and he tried to
sleep through his trials.

Jonah needed an attitude change. Can you identify with
that? Perhaps you are sick and tired of your spouse, your
children, or your co-workers. You might even be sick and
tired of being sick and tired! Often, we find ourselves nursing
a bad attitude, and we desperately need an adjustment. God
knows exactly how to bring about that necessary change in
our lives.

On the boat, the mariners threw out everything precious
to them, including the cargo that represented their wages.
When our lives are threatened, things have a way of becoming
unimportant. Things that we considered essential before no
longer seem significant. In light of eternity, our priorities
change; holding onto life becomes the most important
thing. Unwittingly, Jonah sets himself up to lose everything,

including his life. **Proverbs 24:33-34** aptly describes Jonah:

> *Yet a little sleep, a little slumber, a little folding*
> *of the hands to sleep: So shall thy poverty come*
> *as one that travelleth; and thy want as an*
> *armed man.*

Instead of praying, Jonah slept. Even the pagan Phoenician sailors prayed, but not Jonah, a member of God's chosen people! We find the apostle Peter having the same problem in the Garden of Gethsemane. Just before Jesus' arrest, He asks Peter to stay awake and pray with Him; but Peter cannot keep his eyes open. After that, we are told that he followed the Lord from afar off, even though he professed his undying loyalty to Jesus. Peter's lack of prayer put him in the enemy's crosshairs, and as we know, he ended up denying the Lord. Jonah had the same problem. He lost touch with God and quickly became Satan's target.

> *So the shipmaster came to him, and said unto*
> *him, What meanest thou, O sleeper? arise, call*
> *upon thy God, if so be that God will think upon*
> *us, that we perish not.*   **Jonah 1:6**

An interesting saying, appropriate to Jonah's situation, originated during World War II: "There are no atheists in foxholes." This basically means that when faced with extremely dangerous or fearful circumstances, everyone will turn to a higher power for help. Though Jonah's shipmates prayed to idols, when their situation seemed hopeless, they begged Jonah to call upon the living and true God.

Jonah was the only one on the ship who truly knew how to

pray, but he was asleep. The other sailors were busy praying to their little gods and throwing things overboard. The captain of the ship came to Jonah out of desperation. He was probably thinking, "What is wrong with you? How can you sleep through this? Snap out of it!"

In order for Jonah to pray appropriately, a few things needed to happen. First, he needed to confess his sins. Why? Because **Isaiah 59:1-2** says:

> *Behold, the LORD's hand is not shortened, that*
> *it cannot save; neither his ear heavy, that it*
> *cannot hear: But your iniquities have separated*
> *between you and your God, and your sins have*
> *hid his face from you, that he will not hear.*

We all deal with sin in our lives; but when we confess our sins, God will forgive us!

Next, Jonah needed to repent. God requires our repentance in addition to confession. We must turn from our sin, not just admit our mistakes. Jonah needed to do both of these things, but he refused and lost the power of prayer. Some call **1 John 1:9** the Christian's bar of soap. We need cleansing every single day. **Psalm 66:18** says,

> *"If I regard iniquity in my heart, the Lord will*
> *not hear me."*

John writes that God does not listen to those who hold sin in their hearts. If Jonah had tried to pray without a change of heart, God would have turned a deaf ear to him. Jonah's refusal to confess and repent prevented him from coming before God.

> *And they said everyone to his fellow, Come,
> and let us cast lots, that we may know for
> whose cause this evil is upon us. So they cast
> lots, and the lot fell upon Jonah.*   **Jonah 1:7**

Casting lots was an ancient method of equal selection, sort of like flipping a coin. In this case, as the lot falls to Jonah, we see God's finger upon him. The Bible confirms that our sins will find us out. **Proverbs 16:33** says,

> *"The lot is cast into the lap; but the whole
> disposing thereof is of the Lord."*

The guilty will always be found out. For Jonah, that meant the lot fell right on him. Do you remember Achan? He stole from the spoils of Jericho even though the Lord commanded the people to take nothing. Achan thought he was safe because he had stolen in secret. But when Joshua walked down the line, he stopped at Achan and said, "You are the man!" Achan's sin caused the deaths of his entire family. Next, think of King David. When David took Bathsheba and had her husband killed, Nathan confronted him, telling the story of the rich man who slaughtered the poor man's beloved lamb. David listened to Nathan and said, "The man who has done this shall surely die!"
Nathan said, "David, you are the man!" David immediately realized his sin before the Lord.

Near the end of the 19th century, a man named Frank Shaw captained a ship around Cape Horn. The ship's crew mutinied, shot Captain Shaw, and threw him overboard where his body landed on a sheet of ice. When they returned home, they said that the captain had died of an illness, and they had buried him at sea. The sailors made a pact never to breathe a word about the murder they committed. However, in 1910, an iceberg drifted close by a port in Chile. They sent a team carrying explosives to the iceberg, planning to destroy it in order to prevent damage to their ports. When the team arrived at the iceberg, they found Frank Shaw preserved in the ice with a bullet hole through his head. Even though forty years had passed, the men responsible for the mutiny were hanged. This story illustrates two truths found in Jonah: first, the enemy often makes it seem as though we are getting away with our sin. Second, and most importantly, always remember that your sins will find you out.

> *Then said they unto him, Tell us, we pray thee, for whose cause this evil is upon us; What is thine occupation? and whence comest thou? what is thy country? and of what people art thou?* **Jonah 1:8**

In the midst of this storm, the mariners now question Jonah. They know that he is responsible for their crisis, and they want to know why.

> *"And he said unto them, I am an Hebrew; and I fear the LORD, the God of heaven, which hath made the sea and the dry land."* **Jonah 1:9**

When Jonah explains that he is a God-fearing Jew, you can imagine what the mariners are thinking! No doubt they thought Jonah was crazy for running from a God who created the sea that threatened to overcome them! Jonah defines God as the one who created the earth, and in verse 10 the sailors begin to realize how awesome He is.

> *Then were the men exceedingly afraid, and said unto him, Why hast thou done this? For the men knew that he fled from the presence of the LORD, because he had told them.*
> **Jonah 1:10**

The sailors greatly feared God, as Jonah should have done in the first place. He was being rebuked by a bunch of hardened sailors. These heathen, pagan men could see right through Jonah. It is humbling to receive a rebuke from an unbeliever! As Christians, we strive to follow the Word of God; and suddenly someone at work calls you out saying, "What is with you? I thought you were a Christian?" These reprimands should strike home! When heathens start rebuking us, we have surely strayed from God's path.

> *Then said they unto him, What shall we do unto thee, that the sea may be calm unto us? for the sea wrought, and was tempestuous. And he said unto them, Take me up, and cast me forth into the sea; so shall the sea be calm unto you: for I know that for my sake this great tempest is upon you.* **Jonah 1:11-12**

Those aboard the ship panic as the storm becomes increasingly violent. Charles Spurgeon once said, "God never allows His children to sin successfully." Whom the Lord loves, He chastens. Now, God begins to chasten Jonah.

Though Jonah tells the men to cast him overboard, we must

be careful to avoid looking at Jonah as a martyr. Remember, he would rather die than obey God's will. A true martyr is willing to die obeying God's will. In **1 Kings 19:1-5,** Elijah faces a similar situation:

> *And Ahab told Jezebel all that Elijah had done, and withal how he had slain all the prophets with the sword. Then Jezebel sent a messenger unto Elijah, saying, So let the gods do to me, and more also, if I make not thy life as the life of one of them by to morrow about this time. And when he saw that, he arose, and went for his life, and came to Beersheba, which belongeth to Judah, and left his servant there. But he himself went a day's journey into the wilderness, and came and sat down under a juniper tree: and he requested for himself that he might die; and said, It is enough; now, O LORD, take away my life; for I am not better than my fathers. And as he lay and slept under a juniper tree, behold, then an angel touched him, and said unto him, Arise and eat.*

In this passage, we see Elijah feeling sorry for himself and asking the Lord to take his life. Elijah wanted the easy way out. So many people follow this path. Instead of allowing God to bless them, they wallow in self-pity. Jonah should have confessed his sins. He should have surrendered. Think of the witness he could have been to these men! Not Jonah, though. His stubbornness causes him to undergo a severe trial.

In the book of **Acts 27:23-26,** we find the apostle Paul in a shipwreck. While the wind and waves pound and batter the ship, verses 23-24 say:

> *For there stood by me this night the angel of God, whose I am, and whom I serve, saying, Fear not, Paul; thou must be brought before Caesar: and, lo, God hath given thee all them that sail with thee.*

Paul was the opposite of Jonah. He exhibited faith and courage. He knew that the Lord would protect everyone on the ship and not a single person would perish. Unlike Paul, Jonah did not listen to the Lord. Where was his obedience? His courage?

Though Jonah admitted he should be cast overboard, the mariners had more honor than that! In fairness to Jonah, they tried desperately to stay in control of the ship. He had paid for his passage, and they tried in vain to find a solution other than casting Jonah into the sea. Of course, God had another plan.

> *"Nevertheless the men rowed hard to bring it to the land; but they could not: for the sea wrought, and was tempestuous against them."*
> **Jonah 1:13**

Remember, verse five says that the men threw everything overboard. With their lightened load, they try desperately to get to land. They did everything in their power to save both the ship and themselves. **Isaiah 64:6** says:

> *But we are all as an unclean thing, and all our*

righteousnesses are as filthy rags; and we all do
fade as a leaf; and our iniquities, like the wind,
have taken us away.

The mariners' futile attempt to reach shore illustrates our helplessness without God. No matter how hard we work, we cannot save ourselves. We are saved by God's grace and by Christ's blood that was shed for us.

Wherefore they cried unto the LORD, and
said, We beseech thee, O LORD, we beseech
thee, let us not perish for this man's life, and lay
not upon us innocent blood: for thou, O LORD,
hast done as it pleased thee.   **Jonah 1:14**

Despite Jonah's disobedience, his story shows one of the greatest revivals in the history of mankind. That revival begins in verse fourteen: these pagan sailors cry out to God, recognizing Him as Lord. We should take comfort in this knowledge! God uses His children through the most unusual and even sinful circumstances. Though Jonah rebelled, God used him as a witness. In the same way, God uses us in every circumstance, whether good or bad.

FIG. 3

*"So they took up Jonah, and cast him forth into
the sea: and the sea ceased from her raging."*
Jonah 1:15

After the sailors plead for God's forgiveness, they cast Jonah overboard. Miraculously, the storm ceases, and the sea becomes like glass! Jonah said this would happen, and it did. The mariners cried out to the Lord and they were saved.

*"Then the men feared the LORD exceedingly,
and offered a sacrifice unto the LORD, and
made vows."*   **Jonah 1:16**

No longer afraid of the storm, the mariners now begin to honor the Lord, and they offer sacrifices and make vows to Him. Their salvation and sacrifice foreshadows the salvation and sacrifice of Nineveh.

God has incredible ways of capturing our attention. We may experience a chastening from the Lord in order to get our lives back on track. When we are dissatisfied, God often allows us to go through difficult situations in order to change our perspective. In **Psalm 112**, we see that He wants us to be happy in His will.

In times of spiritual trials, we must look back to our personal relationship with the Lord. How is our prayer life? Are we experiencing intimacy with Him? Or do we act like we don't need God, and we can do everything on our own? When this happens, God teaches us that we can do nothing without Him. All of the sudden, we find ourselves on our knees, asking for God's mercy. During times like these, God opens our hearts, removing logjams, and allowing His goodness to flow out of us.

Remember what **Ephesians 6:6** says:

> *"Not with eyeservice, as menpleasers; but as the servants of Christ, doing the will of God from the heart."*

God wants us to do His will from our hearts, not seeking the praise of men but seeking the praise of God. This is where Jonah messed up, and he experienced what David wrote of in **Psalm 118:18**.

> *"The LORD has chastened me sore: but He has not given me over unto death."*

> *"Now the LORD had prepared a great fish to swallow up Jonah. And Jonah was in the belly of the fish three days and three nights."*
> **Jonah 1:17**

What a miracle we find in this verse! God prepared and appointed a great fish to swallow Jonah. We often question just how Jonah survived in a fish's actual belly for three whole days and nights. Now, if man can create submarines to last for weeks underwater, God can surely make a creature to swallow Jonah and sustain him for a few days. The truth is, Jonah's giant fish is a miracle; it is supernatural, just like the death and resurrection of Jesus. We believe the fish story just as we believe that Jesus rose from the dead. We cannot prove these things with physical evidence, nor do we need to. We trust God's Word, and that is proof enough.

I believe that God made a fish specifically to swallow Jonah. That is nothing for Him. Many people attempt to find out the exact kind of fish that swallowed Jonah. Forget trying to figure it out! The Lord simply says, "Do you believe it?" When we look to the cross, how can we explain it? Christ died for our sins and rose again on the third day. We believe this in our hearts, and God grants us everlasting life.

As we finish the first chapter of this book, we leave Jonah in a tight spot. When we run from God, we always find ourselves in trouble. In situations like Jonah's, we can harden our hearts and grow bitter, or we can soften our hearts and learn from our struggles.

Does God possess your body and soul, or does He just have a piece of you? He wants us to present our bodies a living sacrifice. God takes our sinful hearts and turns us into something good and beautiful. Often, the most painful circumstances in our lives result in the most spiritual growth. When Joseph's brothers sold him into slavery, he suffered tremendously; but God used it for good. In **Genesis 50:20**, Joseph says,

> *"But as for you, ye thought evil against me; but God meant it unto good, to bring to pass, as it is this day, to save much people alive."*

God uses even the most evil circumstances for His glory. Joseph's brothers tried to kill him, but God eventually used Joseph to save their lives.

We know the outcome of the Book of Jonah. What we need to see is the actual process of his regeneration. When we stop running from God, He accepts us just as the father accepted his prodigal son. As we embrace God's will for our lives, others will see Him working through us.

STUDY NOTES

STUDY NOTES

RUNNING BACK TO GOD

The second chapter of Jonah flows beautifully, imitating the psalms in both style and content. First, it consists almost entirely of Jonah's praise to God. Many psalmists, like David, wrote from caves while they endured extreme hardships. In a similar fashion, Jonah prays to God from the belly of the fish, his own cave, so to speak. Jonah's trial teaches him some incredible things about the Lord, and he begins to praise God for delivering him from the sea. Jonah's rescue shows us the theme for the whole book—God's salvation of His people.

You never know what lies ahead when you run from God. In Jonah's case, a giant fish swallowed him alive! Now, I am sure that Jonah expected to die in the ocean; in fact, he probably panicked even more when a giant fish opened its mouth to swallow him. In reality, though, God sent the great fish to become Jonah's life preserver for three days and three nights. That day, Jonah witnessed God's miraculous work first hand.

Trying to understanding miracles is an exercise in futility. Usually, the people who insist on picking miracles apart do so because they lack the Spirit of God. Once the Holy Spirit has touched our hearts, we find it easy to believe the unbelievable. The biggest miracle of all is how God changes our lives; He knows exactly what we need to get back on track. No one illustrates this better than Jonah does!

God gave Jonah just enough rope to see his need for the Lord but not enough to hang himself. God has a way of letting things fall apart as He begins to chasten us. He let Jonah get into a scary place, and He often does the same with us. Remember that God loves His children enough to care what happens to us. When Jonah ran, God went after him; He always goes after His children.

The middle of the ocean can be a scary place! As a surfer, I can somewhat relate. I remember sitting on my board, far from shore, looking out over the peaceful water. All of the sudden, a porpoise swims by, and I start to panic, thinking it might grab me and pull me under. Now, a porpoise is one thing, but what if a shark swims by and mistakes you for a seal! Imagine Jonah's situation: no surfboard to cling to, treading water and watching the ship sail away from him. What would you do in his situation? I know what I would do! I would cry out, "Oh, God, save me!" What Jonah did not know was that God had already prepared a safe place for him, even in the midst of the sea.

> *"Then Jonah prayed unto the LORD his God out of the fish's belly."*   **Jonah 2:1**

Some readers see the word "then" at the beginning of verse

one and infer that Jonah waited for a full three days and nights before he began to pray—as if Jonah sat in full rebellion, arms folded, stubbornly refusing to call upon God. I do not see Jonah that way. I believe he started praying as soon as he entered the ocean, knowing that his sins had caught up with him. When we pray, things begin to change. God's timing is not always our timing, and He chose to wait those three days and nights for His own purposes.

FIG. 4

Put yourself in Jonah's present situation. The belly of the fish is dark and wet, with digestive juices flowing. If the fish were a mammal, such as a whale, the animal's body temperature would be around 98.6 degrees, making Jonah hot and humid. Undoubtedly, there was an atrocious smell adding to Jonah's misery. The scripture says that he had weeds wrapped about his head. What a rude awakening for Jonah! Every one of us has a different breaking point. For the prodigal son in **Luke 15**, it was when he found himself talking and eating with the pigs. He thought to himself, "What am I doing here? I used to have money and a future. Now I have nothing." God wants us to see His goodness and salvation.

God's goodness brings us to repentance. Sometimes we stray from the path, but God still knocks on our hearts. He says,

"I still want to be a part of your life. I gave My Son for you, and you do not have to go through this pain anymore. I have been trying to get your attention because I love you."

How can you help but weep when God apprehends your heart? We say, "But God, how can you love me? Look at all the wrong I have done!" God's great love brings us to our knees.

Prayer

God requires us to pray, especially in times of trial. His Word says that we have not because we ask not. This is often true. We forget that prayer is one of our most important callings. However, sometimes we pray insincerely. In **James 4:3** we are told,

> *"Ye ask, and receive not, because ye ask amiss, that ye may consume it upon your lusts."*

Our prayers consist of bargains. We say, "God, if You can just get me this car, I will bring people to church." We cannot wheel and deal with God, though we often try. Other times we fail to pray because we assume that God will not hear us. We convince ourselves that we are not worthy enough, and our minds spin with self-accusations: we have not walked closely with the Lord, we have not gone to church lately, or we have not been in the Word. When this happens, we start losing our prayer lives, and we allow the enemy to gain a foothold with his lies. Nevertheless, God is gracious, and he constantly draws us to Himself saying, "Come and cast your cares upon Me because I love you. Confess your sins, and I will take them from you." **Isaiah 59:1-2** says:

> *Behold, the LORD's hand is not shortened, that it cannot save; neither his ear heavy, that it cannot hear: But your iniquities have separated between you and your God, and your sins have hid his face from you, that he will not hear.*

Sin hinders our prayers, and we must deal with it before it prevents us from walking closely with the Lord. **Psalm 66:18** says,

> *"If I regard iniquity in my heart, the Lord will not hear me."*

Be careful that you confess your sins and come before the Lord with a heart that genuinely desires to hear from Him.

In verse two, we find Jonah at the breaking point, and he cries out to God in his pain:

> *And said, I cried by reason of mine affliction unto the Lord, and he heard me; out of the belly of hell cried I, and thou heardest my voice.*   **Jonah 2:2**

I have said before that God has a nutcracker for every kind of nut. Jonah was a hard one, but his experience with the whale cracked him easily! What hardship do you need to suffer before you crack? God knows exactly how to reduce us to a place where we submit to Him.

Many of us pray constantly for loved ones to arrive at this place of brokenness. Maybe you are praying for a spouse or a close friend. I believe that the greatest prayer we can make in this situation is to beg the Lord to do whatever it takes to bring that sinner to his knees. The Lord will deal with him in a powerful way, all to His glory.

Sometimes God allows afflictions that cause us to cry out to Him. David certainly experienced this! In **Psalm 119:67** David says,

> *"Before I was afflicted I went astray: but now have I kept thy word."*

A few verses later in **Psalm 119:71**, he comes to this conclusion:

> *"It is good for me that I have been afflicted; that I might learn thy statutes."*

The fish was Jonah's affliction. God took drastic measures, and Jonah cried out to Him. Even though Jonah tried to go his own way, the Lord said, "No!" He brought about the exact circumstances necessary to break Jonah's stubbornness and put him on the path of righteousness.

1 Peter 3:12 tells us:

> *For the eyes of the Lord are over the righteous,*
> *and his ears are open unto their prayers: but*
> *the face of the Lord is against them that do*
> *evil.*

Our greatest comfort as believers should be that God inclines his ear to our prayers. Charles Spurgeon said, "He who learns to pray has learned the secret to a holy and happy life." We must ask him, "Lord, teach us to pray. Teach us to cry out to You."

Do not forget, however, that belief is a vital aspect of prayer. When we ask of God, we must have confidence that He will answer. We must have faith! Lack of belief will make us lose our bearing. Prayer gives us direction from the Lord. Even if all we can muster is a short, simple prayer, we must cry out to the Lord in faith.

Before we go further, we must question Jonah's motives. Is he in the Lord's will at this point? Is he ready to bring the gospel to Nineveh or does he simply wish for liberation from his smelly, wet surroundings? We must answer this next question honestly. In Jonah's situation, would you not pray the same way? When afflictions come we often say, "Lord, just get me out of here!" I think Jonah just wanted to get out of that fish. Eventually, the Lord will bring Jonah to the breaking point, but he is not there quite yet.

Next, is asking God to remove our affliction really the right prayer? When David met Goliath on the battlefield, he did not pray, "Lord, remove this giant. This task is impossible!" Instead, David faced a nine-foot tall, fully armed, experienced warrior. David was probably only in his teens at the time, but he had confidence in the Lord. He sprinted towards Goliath with his sling in hand and killed the giant with one stone. David proclaimed, "It is the Lord who did this!" God guided the rock, like a missile, right between Goliath's eyes. In human eyes, David's fight was futile, but we know that all things are possible with God! He carries His children through every situation, no matter how difficult.

Often we wonder, "Why, God? Why must I experience these afflictions in the first place?" God allows trials in order to strengthen our walk with Him. Jonah went through a major trial in his life, and God allowed it. **James 1:2-3** says,

> *"My brethren, count it all joy when ye fall into divers temptations; Knowing this, that the trying of your faith worketh patience."*

Why should we count hardships as joy? It seems foolish to find happiness in adversity. However, without trials we would never understand how big our God is. He is bigger than any situation we could ever come across.

Have you ever witnessed a friend going through a trial and

thought, "How are they ever going to get through that?" We must realize that God can remove our afflictions as quickly as He wants. He allows it because trials serve a purpose in our lives. Remember, God knows what we need and when we need it. He allows nothing to happen without it first passing before His throne. Yes, God allows both blessings and trials in our lives, but He always has our good in mind.

In Scripture, we see example after example of God's children dealing with trials. The apostle Paul eventually began to embrace his trials, as did James. These were true men of God! When God saves us, we become His children, completely surrendered to His will. We give Him charge of our lives, including our trials. When afflictions come into your life, do not pray for escape. Instead, pray that the Lord will reveal His love through even the most difficult circumstances.

Was Jonah Dead?

Many bible scholars debate over what happened during Jonah's three days and three nights in the belly of the fish. While most people believe that Jonah remained alive in the fish's belly, some interpreters think he physically died. The Bible does not conclusively state this, but it is an interesting question. Jonah says, *"Out of the belly of hell cried I."* In Hebrew, hell is Sheol, the world of the dead. Jonah is saying, "I was in the world of the dead, and I cried out to God."

Let's look at some biblical examples of Sheol. Jesus gives an eye opening account about this world of the dead in

Luke 16:19-31. He tells us that hell is made up of two compartments: one for the righteous dead and one for the unrighteous. The first is Abraham's Bosom, and the second is a place of torment. Between these two compartments is a great gulf that no one can cross. Jesus visited this place after He died on the cross, before His resurrection.

Peter tells us that during these three crucial days Jesus came and preached to those who were in Sheol. **Isaiah 51:14** says,

> *"The captive exile hasteneth that he may be*
> *loosed, and that he should not die in the pit,*
> *nor that his bread should fail."*

In other words, Jesus set these captives free and they followed Him. In **Matthew 27:52**, we see graves opening and people who had died walking around. Jesus took these freed captives with Him to heaven, but first many people saw them in the flesh.

Abraham's Bosom and Paradise are the same place. On the cross, one of the thieves asked Jesus to remember him; and Jesus promised that the thief would be with Him in Paradise that very day. However, because of Jesus' sacrifice, Paradise is now empty; its inhabitants are in heaven. Now only one compartment remains: Hell. This is the holding tank for those who died without believing in Christ.

Strangely enough, Jesus taught more about hell then He

did about heaven. This is a literal place of eternal torment. **Revelation 20:15** says,

> *"And whosoever was not found written in the*
> *book of life was cast into the lake of fire."*

This lake of fire is called Gehenna, where Jesus says there will be weeping and gnashing of teeth. Gehenna is also called 'outer darkness'. This Lake of Fire will burn continuously for all eternity. This terrible fate awaits those who die without Christ.

In conclusion, chapter two does not reveal if Jonah actually died in the fish's belly. Think about which is the greater miracle, keeping Jonah alive in a fish's belly for three days and nights, or raising him from the dead?[i]

Whether Jonah died or not, he certainly came out of the experience a different man. His perspective on the lost, those without hope, changed. He may or may not have died physically, but he did die to himself. God wants each of us to experience this. We must die to ourselves and live for Him. That is the key to our Christian walk.

---

i If Jonah did physically die during his ordeal in the fish's belly, it would even more closely parallel Christ's death, burial, and resurrection. Matthew 12:40, "For as Jonas was three days and three nights in the whale's belly; so shall the Son of man be three days and three nights in the heart of the earth."

God's Purpose

God's plan for us does not end with salvation. That is only the beginning! In Jonah's case, God had a great purpose for saving him. He wanted to use Jonah to save Nineveh. God's work in our lives is never merely to save us from a sticky situation. God saves us in order to make us instruments by which He blesses others. He delivers us and gives us a testimony to share His light.

Our personal testimonies are very powerful. Do you share yours with family, or friends, or those you work with? God has changed our hearts and lives, and we should not keep that blessing to ourselves. God has such a compassion for the lost. The people of Nineveh were in a severely sinful state. They immersed themselves in a pagan culture that offered no chance of salvation. Spiritually, Nineveh was similar to Sodom and Gomorrah, utterly dark and evil. God needed Jonah to share His love with a hopeless people. Without God's intervention, how could the Ninevites receive eternal life? They needed Him desperately.

Jonah's story should challenge us to share the gospel. As believers, we know that hell exists and that unbelievers go there daily. Do you believe what Jesus said about hell in the Bible? Our knowledge of hell should drastically change our perspective. We have a new purpose to share the Gospel with others. We should have an urgency to share Jesus' love with them. Those around us do not have to experience this place of the dead. There is hope. They can experience Jesus' love today.

> *For thou hadst cast me into the deep, in the midst of the seas; and the floods compassed me about: all thy billows and thy waves passed over me.* **Jonah 2:3**

Sitting inside the belly of the fish, Jonah begins to accept God's discipline. He says to God, "I know that You did this. You cast me into the deep, in the midst of the seas." Jonah did not blame the sailors who threw him overboard. He realized that his chastening was from the Lord. We can learn from this lesson! How many times are we quick to blame someone else for our wrongdoings? We blame our parents, or our spouse, or our kids when all God wants is to have our full attention. To his credit, Jonah came to this all-important realization. The Lord had allowed this trial into his life for a reason, and Jonah was ready to listen.

The author of **Hebrews 12:11** tells us this:

> *Now no chastening for the present seemeth to be joyous, but grievous: nevertheless afterward it yieldeth the peaceable fruit of righteousness unto them which are exercised thereby.*

We understand the first part of this verse—no one likes to be chastened! However, we must pay special attention to the second part of this verse. God chastens us in order to bring forth fruit from our lives. If this is true, then we must look at how we respond to God's chastening. Do we despise it? Do we fight it? Do we allow ourselves to become discouraged? Do we resist it? Or do we submit to it, and allow God to build us up?

When we surrender to God's discipline, He strengthens us. He knows that we have trials ahead, and He prepares us accordingly. God does this because He loves His children and wants each one of us to finish the race well. In doing so, He continually brings forth fruit from our lives. Here, Jonah experiences God's love for His children firsthand.

> *Then I said, I am cast out of thy sight; yet I will look again toward thy holy temple. The waters compassed me about, even to the soul: the depth closed me round about, the weeds were wrapped about my head.* **Jonah 2:4-5**

In these two verses, we find Jonah's turning point. He begins by acknowledging the obvious: "I am cast out of thy sight." Ironically, Jonah was running from God. More than anything, he *wanted* to get out of God's sight. Now, alone in the belly of the fish, Jonah turns from his disobedience saying, "I will look again toward thy holy temple." He no longer desires to run from God; instead, he wants to be near Him. This is only the beginning of his confession, but he continues throughout the chapter:

> *I went down to the bottoms of the mountains;*

> *the earth with her bars was about me*
> *forever: yet hast thou brought up my life from*
> *corruption, O LORD my God. When my soul*
> *fainted within me I remembered the LORD:*
> *and my prayer came in unto thee, into thine*
> *holy temple.*   **Jonah 2:6-7**

Jonah continues praying in verses six and seven, recognizing that he got what he asked for, so to speak. God cast him out and gave Jonah a glimpse of life without Him. Look where Jonah ended up. His downward descent began at Joppa and continued as he went down into the ship. From there, he descended into the sea and into belly of the fish. Jonah eventually went down to Sheol, the lowest of the lows. We ask ourselves, how could this happen? God allowed Jonah to get what he wanted; however, Jonah ended up not liking his own plan. Many times, we want certain things, and we refuse to believe that God knows better than we do. God alone knows what we need, and we must learn to trust Him.

Whether we recognize it or not, when we turn away from God, we head downward. If we refuse to walk with the Lord today, we will take a spiritual turn for the worse. However, if we have a right standing with the Lord, he brings us up from the depths of our sin. In Jonah's case, God allowed severe circumstances before Jonah finally began to turn to Him. Finally, at his breaking point, Jonah says, "Yet hast thou brought up my life from corruption." The Lord was raising Jonah up.

When God raises us up out of our old lifestyles, we find His guidance very encouraging, especially those of us who have children. The Lord gives us a command to raise our children up in His ways. We promise to dedicate our children to the Lord, and we fulfill that promise by reading Bible stories at bedtime, by praying, or by singing worship songs in the car. We pour our hearts into them, and they receive the Word. However, as our children grow older, the world begins to knock at the door. It can get especially nerve-wracking when your child becomes a teenager. We find ourselves at our wit's end, crying out to God, "Lord, help me with my son, my daughter! I am trying to do my best, Lord." Do not give up! Just as the Lord cared for Jonah, He cares for you and your children, and He will never forsake you.

In **2 Timothy 3:15**, the Apostle Paul wrote to young pastor Timothy:

> *And that from a child thou hast known the holy scriptures, which are able to make thee wise unto salvation through faith which is in Christ Jesus.*

Timothy's mother and grandmother loved the Lord, and they poured that love into Timothy, teaching him Scripture from a very early age. When God pours His Word into us, it stays in our hearts and lives. Even when you feel like giving up, keep pouring God's love into your children. He will water the seed you have planted and cause it to grow in His own time.

Though Jonah ran from God, he ended up right back at the temple of the Lord. He prayed, "*and [his] prayer came in unto thee, into thine holy temple.*" Where else could he go? The Bible says to train up your children in the ways of the Lord, and when they are older, they will not depart from it. They might fall away for a time, but as with Jonah, God's Word will always go with them to lead them back.

Inside the fish, Jonah remembered his Scripture. I believe he was thinking of **1 Kings 8:38-40**. This is King Solomon's dedication prayer for Israel. Solomon says:

> *What prayer and supplication soever be made by any man, or by all thy people Israel, which shall know every man the plague of his own heart, and spread forth his hands toward this house: Then hear thou in heaven thy dwelling place, and forgive, and do, and give to every man according to his ways, whose heart thou knowest; (for thou, even thou only, knowest the hearts of all the children of men;) That they may fear thee all the days that they live in the land which thou gavest unto our fathers.*

Jonah remembered these scriptures and gave a simple prayer in the same manner. God heard Jonah and forgave him. The most important thing to take away from this lesson is that Jonah took the time to make things right with the Lord. He confessed, he repented, and he praised God. Undoubtedly, Jonah feared his circumstances, but he looked up toward heaven and recalled the promises of God. Remember **Isaiah 26:3** which says,

> *"Thou wilt keep him in perfect peace, whose mind is stayed on thee: because he trusteth in thee."*

Jonah's mind was stayed on Christ, just as ours must be. In **Psalm 5:2-3**, David cries out to the Lord:

> *Hearken unto the voice of my cry, my King, and my God: for unto thee will I pray. My voice shalt thou hear in the morning, O LORD; in the morning will I direct my prayer unto thee, and will look up.*

Jonah and David realized that keeping their eyes on Jesus was vital to their walk with Him. David says that he begins his day by "looking up" to the Lord. Likewise, we should begin and end our days by looking to the Lord.

> *They that observe lying vanities forsake their own mercy. But I will sacrifice unto thee with the voice of thanksgiving; I will pay that that I have vowed. Salvation is of the LORD.*
> **Jonah 2:8-9**

Jonah recollects what he has learned from his experience.

He says that those who "observe lying vanities forsake their own mercy." In other words, when we do not listen to the Lord or His Word, we abandon our hope of salvation. How many of us waste hours at a time pursuing earthly goals? Our prayer should be, "Lord, show us how to live our lives for You, instead of spending it on meaningless pursuits." This does not mean we cannot enjoy playing sports or watching a movie. It means we must place God first, seeking His face on a daily basis, moment by moment. This is what it truly means to walk with the Lord.

Why are we so attracted to meaningless activity? Voices everywhere vie for our attention. The media, family, friends, and especially Satan influence us daily. God wants to replace those voices with His Word. In order to hear Him, we must apply ourselves to Scripture, where the Lord speaks to us directly.

As soon as Jonah stopped listening to God, he deceived himself into accepting three major errors. First, he deceived himself into believing that he could run away from God. King David proclaimed in **Psalm 139:8**,

> *"If I ascend up into heaven, thou art there: if I make my bed in hell, behold, thou art there."*

We cannot run from God. Where would we go? He is everywhere.

Secondly, Jonah mistakenly believed he knew better than

God did. God sent Jonah to Nineveh because He knew Jonah needed that experience. Jonah rebelled because he thought he knew better than God did. Nobody knows what is better for us than God does. He always has our best interests at heart. Finally, Jonah's third error was thinking he could find happiness apart from God. **Psalm 144:15** says,

> *"Happy are the people whose God is their LORD."*

We never find true happiness apart from God. As Jonah ponders his circumstances, he sees the error of his ways and begins yielding to the Lord. He says, *"But I will sacrifice unto thee with the voice of thanksgiving; I will pay that that I have vowed. Salvation is of the Lord."* Jonah says he will offer sacrifices, and he gives thanks to the Lord. Once again, we see the similarity between Jonah and the prodigal son in **Luke 15:17-18:**

> *And when he came to himself, he said, How many hired servants of my father's have bread enough and to spare, and I perish with hunger! I will arise and go to my father, and will say unto him, Father, I have sinned against heaven, and before thee.*

When we find ourselves in trouble, the smartest thing we can do is run back to God. In his brokenness, Jonah runs back to God and openly confesses his sin. What an important lesson for us! King David also had a similar experience. He was deep in sin and kept tossing and turning, while his guilt was eating him alive. David stubbornly held on to his sin until finally in **Psalm 32:5**, he proclaimed:

> *I acknowledged my sin unto thee, and mine iniquity have I not hid. I said, I will confess my transgressions unto the LORD; and thou forgavest the iniquity of my sin.*

Until we acknowledge and confess our sin, we will continue to wrestle with God. Often, we know our actions are sinful, and we continue doing wrong anyway. As children of God, we cannot continually sin and experience true happiness at the same time. Our sins will make us miserable and keep us awake at night. Worst of all, our constant sinning not only hurts us, it also hurts those around us. We desperately need the Lord's forgiveness to wash us completely clean. He is the only One who can set us free and place us back into fellowship with Him.

Once we respond to God's great love, our gratitude toward Him grows. We find ourselves open to receiving whatever He has for us. God always initiates; we are the responders. God says to us, "I want to bless you. Cry out to Me." The more we cry out to Him, the more He blesses us. In this chapter, Jonah starts to do just that. He begins to forsake his own ways for the Lord's ways.

In his flesh, Jonah hated the Ninevites. He said in his heart, "I am a Hebrew and I stick with my own. I hate the Assyrians!"

However, as he turns toward the Lord, Jonah finally begins to see things God's way, and he responds to God's love and blessing. Now that Jonah has repented and refocused, He is ready to go to the Ninevites and deliver God's message. **Psalm 66:13-14** says:

> *I will go into thy house with burnt offerings:*
> *I will pay thee my vows, Which my lips have*
> *uttered, and my mouth hath spoken, when I*
> *was in trouble.*

When you think about it, Jonah should have died in the sea. The crew cast Jonah overboard, far from shore, in a terrible storm. Nevertheless, God had another plan. He not only spared Jonah's life by sending the great fish, but He gave Jonah a second chance.

Now, Jonah repented of his sin, but still faced the problem of actually escaping from the fish's belly. Jonah knew his situation was overwhelming, but he made the decision to let God handle this one. He knew he could not escape on his own. Jonah said, "I am not going to get out of this on my own. Salvation is of the Lord. God delivers, and I will wait on Him." Getting out of the fish could only be a work of God. Jonah could do nothing. The book of Isaiah tells us that our own righteousness is as "filthy rags." This term describes a menstrual cloth. Isaiah uses this graphic language to emphasize our unworthiness and our inability to help ourselves.

When God saves, He does His work in three tenses. First, we have been saved, which is past tense. The book of **John 3:36** tells us this:

> *He that believeth on the Son hath everlasting life: and he that believeth not the Son shall not see life; but the wrath of God abideth on him.*

When you believe in Jesus, you have everlasting life. Second, we are being saved, which is present tense. Christ saves us daily, right up to the present moment. **Ephesians 2:8-10** says:

> *For by grace are ye saved through faith; and that not of yourselves: it is the gift of God: Not of works, lest any man should boast. For we are his workmanship, created in Christ Jesus unto good works, which God hath before ordained that we should walk in them.*

Third, we will be saved, indicating the future tense. When Christ comes again, we will be changed. **1 John 3:2** tells us:

> *Beloved, now are we the sons of God, and it doth not yet appear what we shall be: but we know that, when he shall appear, we shall be like him; for we shall see him as he is.*

This is an amazing revelation! The Lord's work on the cross

completely covers the past, the present, and the future. The key to enjoying this freedom is to cease from our own labors and enter into the Lord's rest. Jonah had nowhere left to run, except back to God. Though Jonah has many trials to come, he is learning. Like Jonah, we never stop learning.

As long as we live in this world, God continues to teach us important lessons. Jonah's major theme is that we must cease from our own labors and enter into God's rest. In fact, this theme makes up the heart of the entire Bible.

FIG. 5

In the story of the prodigal son, we see the father do two things. First, he waits for his son patiently. Then, when he sees his son, he runs to embrace him. Sometimes, we are just like that prodigal son, seeking to get back home and wondering if God will take us back. We do everything we can to escape from the messes we make, but nothing works. Then, here is God our Father, running to embrace us. He cannot wait to receive us and restore us. When we turn our hearts to Him, He says, "I want to show myself strong towards you."

Consistent Bible Reading

I cannot stress this enough: Jonah's remembrance of Scripture helped him through his hour of trial. Do we read the paper? Magazines? Watch the news? All of these mediums can be seriously depressing and full of the corruption in society today. None of these things truly edify us. We must have the Word of God. It is our daily defense against the pull of the world. In **John 14:26,** Jesus said:

> *But the Comforter, which is the Holy Ghost,*
> *whom the Father will send in my name, he*
> *shall teach you all things, and bring all things*
> *to your remembrance, whatsoever I have said*
> *unto you.*

Jesus wanted to make sure we understood why He sent the Holy Spirit to inhabit us. One of His purposes is to help us remember the things we have read and learned in the Bible. If we do not immerse ourselves in God's Word, we may get lost when we experience trials. We will have nothing for the Holy Spirit to bring to our remembrance.

God's word is our spiritual diet. When we read regularly and take in God's Word, He uses it to strengthen us. We need to take in Scriptures just like we need to eat. If we only feed ourselves once or twice a week, we will eventually starve. Some believers only open their Bibles on Sunday, or perhaps on Wednesday. Feeding ourselves spiritually only twice a week is not a healthy diet. We must feed our spirit every single day.

In **Matthew 11:28-29** Jesus said:

> *Come unto me, all ye that labor and are*
> *heavy laden, and I will give you rest. Take*
> *my yoke upon you, and learn of me; for I am*
> *meek and lowly in heart: and ye shall find*
> *rest unto your souls.*

Jesus freely offers us rest, and in return, we must learn about Him. This is how God builds us up. If you are having trouble reading God's Word, ask Him to give you a desire for it. Force-feed yourself if you have to, but get into the Word. Most importantly, let it get into you. The Lord will bless you as you seek His Word and meditate upon it. He will make you a man or woman who prospers as you sit at the Master's feet.

> *"And the LORD spake unto the fish, and it*
> *vomited out Jonah upon the dry land."*
> **Jonah 2:10**

Time is up for Jonah! The great fish vomits him out on the shore, and Jonah experiences a work of salvation and deliverance from the Lord. In God's timing, all things are beautiful; although I'm sure that Jonah himself didn't look beautiful. You can imagine how this scene must have looked! A giant fish regurgitates a living man onto the shore. Jonah was a mess—smelly, dirty, and bleached from gastric juices. Nevertheless, he was alive!

Such was Jonah's humble beginning in the Lord's service. A prophet, called by God, all of the sudden belched up on the shore. We see how powerful God really is. His prophets can appear anywhere he pleases. All of the sudden, in the midst of nowhere, there they are.

Jonah has been on a tremendous journey already. He ran away from God. Then the crew of the cargo ship threw Jonah overboard into the dark waters below. A fish swallowed him and he spent three days and nights inside its belly. Now the fish is throwing him up onto the dry land. Jonah is coming back to God in complete humility. God has Jonah's heart. He has given Jonah a new life. Jonah has a new outlook and perspective on everything.

When we have blown it and everything seems to be going wrong, remember that God is working. Keep returning to what you know. When Jonah was in the fish, it just felt like outer darkness. However, God was moving the fish exactly where He wanted Jonah to go. Just as God used the fish, He can also use our circumstances, no matter how unusual or difficult. In addition, God always moves with us. We may say, "I can only see darkness. I am confused and I don't know what is going on." But God knows everything that is happening. Just as God used a fish to position Jonah, God is moving you where you need to be.

The Book of Jonah gives us a picture of the death, burial, and resurrection of Jesus Christ. Salvation is of the Lord. We need God's love and His power working in us desperately. Jonah had to cry out, though. This was his road to recovery, but God is not finished with Jonah yet! As we finish chapter two, Jonah still has a lot to learn, as we all do; but at least he is running back to God.

Are you running toward the Lord, or away from Him? What is going on in your life? Are you truly seeking God and His kingdom for your own life and for your family? We must be honest with ourselves and answer these important questions.

Perhaps you are reading this book and you do not have a real relationship with Jesus Christ. You have tried on your own but have always run into a brick wall. You can receive Him today. There are angels in heaven waiting, anticipating your coming. **Luke 15:7** tells us that angels rejoice when just one sinner comes to salvation. In the story of the prodigal son, the son returned and his father was excited.

The son said, "Father, I have sinned. I am sorry." And his father said, "Kill the fatted calf; let us eat and be merry!" Everyone rejoiced. The father said, "We should make merry and be glad. The brother was lost, and he is alive again; he was lost, and now he is found." Does this describe you today? All you need to do is honestly come to Jesus. Confess your sin, and believe in Him who saved you on the cross. Ask Jesus to come into your life and then begin to live for Him.

Study Notes

Study Notes

CHAPTER 3

RUNNING WITH GOD

We know that Jonah is a running man. In chapter one, he ran *away* from God's call and will for his life. In chapter two, Jonah realizes his sin and runs *back* to God. Now, as we move into the second half of this book, we find Jonah running *with* God. Remember the words of **Amos 3:3**,

> *"Can two walk together, except they be agreed?"*

A huge part of trusting the Lord is obeying Him. We cannot do one without the other. If we trust God, it follows logically that we should obey Him, right? Jonah is going to learn this important lesson and hopefully we will too.

If we look back to the beginning of the Old Testament, we see that Jonah is a type of Israel. You may think, "How is that possible?" But look in **Genesis 12:3** and see God's words to Abraham:

> *"And I will bless them that bless thee: and curse him that curseth thee: and in thee shall all families of the earth be blessed."*

Through Israel, or Abraham, many would come to know the Lord, just as Jonah's witnessing would lead many to the Lord.

In chapter two, God began chastening Jonah, who refused to obey. God used extreme circumstances to turn Jonah around. Remember, Jonah was entering a very dark time in his life. We have all gone through those! It may seem like nothing is going right, and we don't know what is happening; yet we take comfort knowing that God is working. Look at **Romans 8:28.**

> *"And we know that all things work together*
> *for good to them that love God, to them who*
> *are the called according to his purpose."*

Like the prodigal again, Jonah turns around as a result of his circumstances. He comes to his senses and runs back to God. Jonah confesses his sins, and God hears his cry and delivers him. Of course, when Jonah looked back and saw how God had used that great fish as a vessel for his salvation, he was thankful. But I am equally convinced that Jonah said, "No more sitting in a fish's belly for me!" When God disciplines us, we learn our lessons. Like the prodigal, we don't want to go back to our pigsty. Jonah emerged from that fish saying, "I give up! I'll do whatever you want me to do, Lord; I'll go to the Ninevites."

Finally, we reach Nineveh itself: act two of the incredible drama of Jonah, the running man. Now we move away from the sea and instead have the great city as our new backdrop. This scene opens with Jonah, no doubt covered in vomit, sitting on the shore of Nineveh. At last, Jonah is running with God. He has finally committed to doing things God's way. When you really think about it, do we have any other choice? We try our own path, just like Jonah did, but we always fail! Sometimes we just have to learn the hard way before we run with the Lord. Once Jonah submitted, God used him in a huge way. As we continue with this book, we will see God's power through Jonah's preaching!

The first time God brought the children of Israel to the Jordan River, they disobeyed and ended up wandering the wilderness for forty years! The second time they reached the Jordan, God said, "Now what are you going to do? Have you learned your lesson this time?" After four decades and the deaths of an entire generation, they were back to square one. In the same way, Jonah ends up back at square one after his rebellious detour; but, in His time, God makes all things beautiful. Doesn't he? All the trials that we experience work together for God's glory and for our own good.

So here we find Jonah, belched up onto the shores of Nineveh and right back where God wanted him to go in the first place. We looked at this in the previous chapter, but I want to review it. In **Luke 11:29-30**, Jesus said:

> *And when the people were gathered thick together, he began to say, This is an evil generation: they seek a sign; and there shall no sign be given it, but the sign of Jonas the prophet. For as Jonas was a sign unto the Ninevites, so shall also the Son of man be to*

this generation.

Let's face it. Jonah has long remained a target for Bible critics. "You mean you really believe that this man was swallowed by a whale?" Yes, we do! Jesus affirms it, just as he did with Daniel and Adam and Eve. These are not just flukes. They are real people, in real situations. The critics persisted in arguing about the validity of Jonah, but in the 1840s, archaeologists discovered the remains of Nineveh.[i] It blew everyone's mind! Isn't it amazing that many archeologists use the Bible to guide their digs? Why? Because the word of God is true! If we keep digging, we will find truth. Jonah is certainly a spiritual sign, but my question is this: could he also have been a physical sign? There are three historical recordings, dating back to the 1800s, of men being swallowed by great fish. They all emerged bleached— white skin, no hair, and no eyebrows.[ii]

Can you imagine if you were a fisherman, and Jonah suddenly popped out onto the sand? With his colorless skin and seaweed wrapped about him, he certainly would grab your attention! Keep this picture of Jonah in your mind until we actually enter the great city of Nineveh. It is incredible!

Now the Great Commission given in **Matthew 28** and in **Mark 16** says we must preach to all nations, giving them the gospel and baptizing them in the name of the Father, the

---

i For centuries, little was known about the city of Nineveh. Many doubted its very existence until these incredible discoveries occurred, once again proving the Bible's reliability. Over the past 165 years, archaeologists have found incredible amounts of information about Assyrian and Babylonian culture.

ii Edward B. Davis, "A Whale of a Tale: Fundamentalist Fish Stories," American Scientific Affiliation: Perspectives on Science and Christian Faith 43:224-237 (1991), http://www. asa3.org/ASA/PSCF/1991/PSCF12-91Davis.html

Son, and the Holy Spirit. God tells us to make disciples of all men.

As Israel, of course, the church has failed miserably. Before the millennium, I knew a lot of people planning Jesus' return for the year 2000. "Let's see the world saved," they said. "Then Jesus will come back!" Of course, we can't predict or induce Jesus' return. Even with all our technology, we still fail to spread the Word; and more people than ever before are born without hearing a word of the Gospel. Isn't it interesting that the greatest revivals took place both before and after the church was on the scene? We are about to see Jonah's teaching in Nineveh start an awesome revival.

Here, Jonah reminded me of **Isaiah 6:5-8** because after Isaiah was convicted of his sin, he also received his commission. Jonah experienced the same progression that Isaiah did. He was convicted of his sins and was cleansed. Next, he committed his life to the Lord, saying, "Here I am. Send me." Finally, he received his commission. As the Lord spoke, Isaiah heard Him. Do you know why? Because he confessed his sin, and he consecrated his life to the Lord. Now we must ask ourselves these same questions. Have we been convicted? Have we confessed our sin? Have we received God's healing and cleansing? And finally, have we concentrated our lives, as **Romans 12:1** says:

> *I beseech you therefore, brethren, by the mercies of God, that ye present your bodies a living sacrifice, holy, acceptable unto God, which is your reasonable service.*

Then God said, *"Isaiah, go tell this people."* I love that! He commanded, and Isaiah went. But Jonah wasn't so obedient when he got his commission, was he? He took off running the other way, and he paid dearly for his actions. Jonah experienced what I like to call payday. We find out that when we sow to the flesh, we reap corruption and confusion. God wants to bring clarity to our lives. He wants to open our eyes and ears and bless us. All we must do is trust and obey. That's the bottom line.

Jonah fled from God, but we know he wasn't happy. God is going to call Jonah again, and what will he do? Will he foolishly attempt to flee or will he obey God's second call? Check out this next verse:

> *"And the word of the LORD came unto Jonah the second time, saying."* **Jonah 3:1**

I love to read this verse, because it tells me that our God offers second chances. We all need to hear this from time to time. The Lord will speak to you again. Perhaps you've read this book before, but you ignored its teachings. Now you have a divine appointment to hear the Word of the Lord a second time. He will give you a whole new lease on life. You might say "Well, I have already blown it more than twice! " Then I have encouragement for you.

Proverbs 24:16 says,

> *"For a just man falleth seven times, and riseth up again: but the wicked shall fall into mischief."*

Now don't say, "I have fallen five times; I have two more

free errors!" That's not how you look at it. This verse is encouragement that our God will give us a second, third, fourth, or fifth chance. He doesn't work as man does—three strikes, you're out! He doesn't fire you for one mistake and forget you. The Lord speaks to us and encourages us, even when we fail. We are sinners, saved by grace. Who among us has never stumbled? **Romans 3:23** says that we have *all* sinned, yet God remains ready to forgive us and lift us up.

What did God do with Jonah in his rebellion? I will tell you this: the Lord never deserted him or allowed him to be harmed. Our Lord God had control of the storm, control of the sailors, and control of the fish. He was in the midst of everything Jonah endured. Read **Philippians 1:6**,

> *"Being confident of this very thing, that he which hath begun a good work in you will perform it until the day of Jesus Christ."*

God will never, ever give up on you. Isn't that a great comfort? He is a Father who cares for and loves His children unconditionally.

I know some people who say, "I really thought we had our man in Jonah, but he ran away from God and ended up in a mess." He sure did, but the Lord chose Jonah yet a second time! God is just trying to show us that we are unique. We each have particular talents and spiritual gifts. God wants us to use those talents, and He will pursue us until we yield to Him. I love this scripture in **Zechariah 4:9**,

> *"The hands of Zerubbabel have laid the*

*foundation of this house; his hands shall also
finish it."*

When God starts a work, He will finish it. God has already
begun working with and through Jonah, and He is not about
to quit now. **Hebrews 13:5** says it all:

> *"He will never leave us or forsake us."*

A similar beautiful scripture occurs in **Isaiah 43:2**.

> *"When thou passest through the waters, I
> will be with thee."*

When Jonah was thrown into the sea, the Lord was with him.
How He loves us, even in our rebellion! The Lord provided
Jonah with the key to living for Him—dying to self. We have
already talked about Jonah's experience paralleling Jesus'
death, burial, and resurrection. As Christians, we know that
to die is to truly live. **Galatians 2:20** says this:

> *I am crucified with Christ: nevertheless I
> live; yet not I, but Christ liveth in me: and the
> life which I now live in the flesh I live by the
> faith of the Son of God, who loved me, and
> gave himself for me.*

So Jonah received God's call a second time, but this time
he listened. I think the question we must ask ourselves is
this: when we read God's Word, does He speak to us? Most
importantly, do we listen? Many times we read scripture, but
we take nothing away from it. We must seek the Holy Spirit
before studying the Bible, and God will share fresh, personal

lessons from His Word. However, we must beware of the enemies' lies. When we fail, he immediately condemns us saying, "You blew it. God doesn't want you anymore because you went too far this time." Once, I visited a man in the ICU whom I'd known for many years. He was lying there on life support, many of his organs not functioning. He couldn't even talk to us. He did finally open his eyes and recognize me, and I was able to talk to him and pray with him. As we visited, his wife shared that her husband lived in fear for years because he had dabbled in witchcraft prior to his salvation. For years, the enemy tormented him with fears of going to hell. In his heart he was saved, but in his mind he was tormented. Seeing him there, going through such mental struggles, reminded me of **Hebrews 6:4-6**, a scripture that the enemy often tries to use against us:

> *For it is impossible for those who were once enlightened, and have tasted of the heavenly gift, and were partakers of the Holy Ghost, and have tasted the good word of God, and the powers of the world to come, if they shall fall away, to renew them again unto repentance; seeing they crucify to themselves the Son of God afresh, and put him to an open shame.*

How many people have read this scripture and thought, "That's me. I am forsaken. I have blasphemed the Holy Spirit!" These verses have nothing to do with believers. The author of Hebrews is speaking about unbelievers, but God's love is not this way. He is full of compassion. Remember how Jesus spoke to the thief on the cross in **Luke 23:43,**

> *"And Jesus said unto him, Verily I say*

> *unto thee, Today shalt thou be with me in paradise."*

I love how we find examples of Christ's compassion all throughout Scripture. He constantly forgave and restored sinners, just like the thief on the cross. I think Peter is one of the greatest illustrations of this. He had such promise, but he blew it. In his anger, Peter gave in to his flesh and cut the priest's ear off. Additionally, he boasted of his love for the Lord, and then denied Him three times. Man might have rejected Peter for this, but the Lord would not let go of him! After his resurrection, the Lord said to Mary, "Go tell Peter that I am alive; I am risen." Peter was filled with the Holy Spirit and wept over his sins, but he got back with the Lord.

We find similar stories of great men all throughout scripture. They failed God, but He lifted them up and allowed them to become servants for Him. Think of Mark. He served the Lord on the mission field with Paul until he said, "I don't like it out here, I'm going home." So young Mark goes home, yet he ended up writing one of the gospels! What happened? The Lord forgave him, anointed him, and got him back in the saddle again, so to speak. Paul even wrote from prison and said, "Send Mark. I love that brother and he is profitable for the ministry." Again, we see that He is the God of the second, third, fourth, and fifth chances and beyond. Over in **Micah 7:8** we read this:

> *"Rejoice not against me, O mine enemy: when I fall, I shall arise."*

Here is true encouragement from the Lord. He constantly says to us, "Listen, I love you and I glory in using imperfect beings to accomplish my perfect will." Remember **1 John 1:9**, the Christian's bar of soap:

> *"If we confess our sins, he is faithful and just*
> *to forgive us our sins, and to cleanse us from*
> *all unrighteousness."*

God forgives and restores, and we must do the same. If our God does that, shouldn't Christians also? Sometimes we encounter tough situations in the church. What about a pastor who commits adultery? Many of us have witnessed that. We have crossed that road, and we have seen God's restorative power.

Remember in the Old Testament how Abraham lied about his wife, saying that she was his sister? I am sure he swallowed hard when he saw Pharaoh take Sarah into his harem, but did the Lord give up on Abraham? Not once. The Lord didn't forsake him, even after Sarah convinced Abraham that she was too old to bear children; and then he fathered Ishmael with Hagar. Yes, he failed, but he later became the father of a great nation. His obedience was imputed unto him as righteousness.

Next we find Jacob: a sneaky wheeler and dealer who lied to his father. The Lord also forgave Jacob. The Lord spoke to him and even wrestled with him, and Jacob became the father of Israel.

Then there is Moses: brought up in a royal home, educated, and smart, but in a fit of anger he killed an Egyptian. Perhaps the Israelites thought, "We can't have a murderer leading God's people!" But God had other plans, and no one but

Moses led God's people out of Egypt. Despite his failure, the Lord allowed him to see the Promised Land before he died. Here is an ex-murderer, yet he's forgiven and he entered into the Promised Land. He was there on the Mount of Transfiguration.

The last example, of course, has to be David: king, warrior, poet, and musician. All of these accomplishments, yet David still had a problem with lust. He took Bathsheba and committed adultery and murder. His actions ruined his family, and his sons rose up against him. He paid dearly for his sins, yet in **Psalm 32:5**, he says:

> *I acknowledged my sin unto thee, and mine iniquity have I not hid. I said, I will confess my transgressions unto the LORD; and thou forgavest the iniquity of my sin.*

David, a man after God's own heart? Really? Yes, because David truly repented, and God forgave him and cleansed him. We thank God for His grace, as the psalmist does in **Psalm 103:4**,

> *"Who redeemeth thy life from destruction; who crowneth thee with lovingkindness and tender mercies."*

God loves and forgives me, but why does he do this? We see the answer below in **I Corinthians 1:27-31**.

> *But God hath chosen the foolish things of the world to confound the wise; and God hath chosen the weak things of the world to*

confound the things which are mighty; And base things of the world, and things which are despised, hath God chosen, yea, and things which are not, to bring to nought things that are: That no flesh should glory in his presence. But of him are ye in Christ Jesus, who of God is made unto us wisdom, and righteousness, and sanctification, and redemption: That, according as it is written, He that glorieth, let him glory in the Lord.

We are warned in the scriptures, especially in Romans, about misusing or abusing God's grace. Yes, we receive amazing grace. Yes, we have God's forgiveness and cleansing, but God help us if we attempt to abuse it! We can't play games with God. He forgives and forgets. Yet in his government, man also reaps what he sows.

> *"Arise, go unto Nineveh, that great city, and preach unto it the preaching that I bid thee."*
> **Jonah 3:2**

Jonah had fallen down, that's for sure! God told him to rise up, and, as verse three tells us, *"Jonah arose, and went unto Nineveh according to the word of the LORD."* Jonah heard God's word and obeyed. I am sure he was toeing the line to avoid ending up back in the fish's belly!

> *"Now Nineveh was an exceeding, great city, of three days journey."* **Jonah 3:3**

Remember from chapter one the sheer power of this Assyrian empire, sixty full miles in circumference! When we look in

Genesis 10:11-12, we see that it wasn't just one city, but many cities strung together. Just walking from one side to the other took three whole days! Though this city contained great wealth, it also contained much evil. There was great idolatry and abomination everywhere. Above all, the Assyrians had no mercy for their enemies. They were ruthless, wicked, and greatly feared. The most exciting thing about this chapter is what God did. He sent Jonah, who learned that God's grace is sufficient for everything. Jonah learns that God will lead us, keep us, and empower us. So Jonah arose, and ran with God. **Romans 10:13-15** talks about going forth with the good news:

> *For whosoever shall call on the name of the Lord shall be saved. How then shall they call on him in whom they have not believed? and how shall they believe in him of whom they have not heard? and how shall they hear without a preacher? and how shall they preach, except they be sent? as it is written, how beautiful are the feet of them that preach the gospel of peace, and bring glad tidings of good things!*

In the same manner, Jonah is going forth into this wicked city carrying the good news.

> *"And Jonah began to enter into the city a day's journey."*   **Jonah 3:4**

He goes in about a third of the way, gathering a crowd by this time. Remember how he looks—bleached and bald— yet he starts preaching. At the end of verse four, He cries out and says, *"Yet forty days and Nineveh shall be overthrown."*

> *"So the people of Nineveh believed God, and*
> *proclaimed a fast and put on sackcloth, from*
> *the greatest of them to the least of them."*

Jonah 3:5

This is an incredible miracle—the greatest revival of all time! Churches plan revival meetings on certain days and hope that many will attend and accept the Lord. Yet it is a true revival when an entire nation turns to the Lord and 600,000 people are saved! As always, the task seems so overwhelming, especially when we try to pray for our own city or country. How do you start that prayer? Well, how do you eat an elephant? You start at the tail and go one bite at a time.

Moses, Gideon, Nehemiah, and Jonathan affected so many with their words and actions, but Jonah doesn't seem to have any obvious advantage. Jonah definitely wasn't an Assyrian. In fact, after his three days in the fish's belly, he probably didn't look like anything the Ninevites had seen before.

Noah never saw a revival like Jonah's. He preached diligently for over one hundred years and only eight people got saved. Jeremiah preached throughout his whole life and never saw one convert! That would be depressing! Can you imagine saying, "All my life and no one came to the Lord, but I steadied on." And Jeremiah did. Now Jonah couldn't foresee what God was going to do. I am sure Jonah thought that he would be impaled or skinned alive, but he went anyway because God called him.

I think there are two reasons, other than God's anointing on his life, that Jonah succeeded. First, Jonah was a real man who went through real trials and emerged with a true heart for the Lord. He didn't have celebrity or fanfare, but he did have a powerful testimony of God's work in his life. Secondly, Jonah was successful because he had a short, simple message. I've heard people call this the K.I.S.S. method. Keep It Simple, Stupid! Jonah's message was only eight words. In Hebrew it is only five! Perhaps Jonah did preach other messages not recorded in scripture, but his God-given message was short and direct.

Perhaps you've gone out witnessing with a group, and you met someone who showed genuine interest in the Word. You got so excited that you jumped into the Scriptures and talked and talked until your friend grabbed your arm and said, "What are you doing? You're into Daniel and eschatology and who knows what else!" That poor person you're witnessing to is sitting there with his mouth open, wondering what in the world you're talking about. Get to the point! "Would you like to receive Jesus Christ into your heart?"

Sometimes, all they want is a short message. People are hurting, and they want hope. They don't need a history lesson or an in-depth study. They want the basics, and they want to receive the Lord. I think we need to show sensitivity. Don't witness on and on *ad nauseum* when someone genuinely desires Christ. We don't need to do the convincing. God can take care of that. People are hurting today; the Holy Spirit is convicting the world of sin. Our job here is to proclaim God's word. Sometimes we are shocked when individuals readily pray for salvation. We think, "Shouldn't this take more time or effort?" Instead of questioning, we should rejoice that the Lord has prepared the hearts of sinners to accept Him!

Jonah proclaimed that Nineveh's downfall would occur in forty days. In scripture, forty is the number of judgment. Remember Noah and how it rained for forty days? Also, the spies in Cana were there for forty days. Israel wandered for forty years, and Jesus fasted in the wilderness for forty days. I think Jonah secretly loved this message because deep down he truly despised the Ninevites. So, of course, he went through the city, proudly giving them the message and sharing of God's love. However, he still didn't like them, and I think he actually enjoyed prophesying their downfall. He probably was thinking, "God is going to wipe the Assyrians out. This is going to be great!"

Jonah also witnessed by sharing his testimony about the living God. Our personal testimonies are very special. The Apostle Paul shared his five times. I have a friend who was instrumental in leading me to a church to hear the gospel and accept Christ. He has been a friend all these years, even before my salvation when we were into drugs and other sins. Twenty years later, my wife and I visited his family, and I started to joke around and share about the old days. He stopped me and quietly told me not to say anything more about it. I was surprised when he asked his kids to leave the room. Then he said, "I have never told them." Here was a respected Christian man, the town fire chief, and he had never shared his testimony with his own children. His kids were off track and into drugs and everything else you can imagine. This respectable man was embarrassed and wanted to hide his past, but I say that the past is God's power working in and through your life. You shouldn't hide it; you should share it because your salvation from those past sins is a miracle. It is the power of God unto salvation. Your children especially need to see that once you were dead, but now you are alive in Christ. My friend didn't want his children to know about his mistakes, but the important thing is that he led me to the Lord. For Jonah, the important thing is that he obeyed God and preached to Nineveh. God did all the rest, didn't He? Revival is the result of God's word being proclaimed. As His word is proclaimed, the Holy Spirit begins to move.

The Bible reveals three main reasons why God created the church. As **Revelations 4:11** says, first and foremost we were created to please the Lord:

> *Thou art worthy, O Lord, to receive glory and honour and power: for thou has created all things, and for thy pleasure they are and were created.*

Next, God created the church that we might edify each other and build one another up in our faith. This is key to our growing in the word of God. Last but not least, God created the church for evangelism. Though this step is extremely important, we cannot accomplish effective evangelism until we have an understanding of the first two reasons: we must have a strong relationship with Christ and with our fellow believers.

God used Jonah as a channel through which to do His life-saving work. The message, of course, was always the same. In **1 Corinthians 1:18**, Paul talks about preaching of the cross:

> *"For the preaching of the cross is to them*
> *that perish foolishness; but unto us which are*
> *saved it is the power of God."*

Jonah didn't come to Nineveh with the wisdom of men; he came with the power of God. Jonah is all about God's power, not the power of men.

Jonah's message stirred the population, and they believed in God. In a poll posted online December 17, 2010, Gallup found that most Americans believe in the existence of God. This doesn't mean that they are saved. **James 2:19** says that *"the devils also believe, and tremble"*! However, we believe in the living and true God who sent His Son to save us. God only asks that we be born again through faith. In Nineveh, Jonah witnessed to the least and to the greatest. Do you know what they did? They immediately repented, from the lowliest beggar to the king of the city. Salvation really is just a prayer away, isn't it? We don't have to attend seminary and jump through all kind of legal hoops. When I heard the gospel for the first time I said, "Wow, that's quick! That's for me. I'll do it." That's how the Ninevites accepted Christ. They were ready to receive. They heard the warning, and they humbled themselves. Immediately, they began to demonstrate their belief by their actions. Notice in verse five, they declared a fast and put on sackcloth, which is rough and painful, signifying their humility and submission to God. From the greatest to the least of them, they showed their humility before God, just like **James 2:18** says:

> *"Show me thy faith without thy works, and*

I will show thee my faith by my works."

Matthew 7:16 carries a similar teaching:

"Ye shall know them by their fruit."

In a crusade years ago, Billy Graham did a great job of comparing our nation to Nineveh. Can you imagine if this country turned to God as Nineveh did? Do you believe that God can do a work in this entire nation? **2 Chronicles 7:14** says:

> *If my people, which are called by my name, shall humble themselves, and pray, and seek my face, and turn from their wicked ways; then will I hear from heaven, and will forgive their sin, and will heal their land.*

We see here that the fate of our country has much to do with us. Our actions and our prayers have a great affect on the world around us. Here we see the whole of Nineveh on its knees, confessing.

> *For the word came unto the king of Nineveh, and he arose from his throne, and he laid his robe from him, and covered him with sackcloth, and sat in ashes.* **Jonah 3:6**

Have you ever been this convicted? When was the last time you mourned over your sins and sat in ashes? I mean this formerly wicked king was truly contrite!

He caused it to be proclaimed and published

> *throughout Nineveh by the decree of the king*
> *and his nobles saying, Let neither man nor*
> *beast, herd nor flock, taste anything: Let them*
> *not feed, nor drink water.*   **Jonah 3:7**

Even the animals had to fast. Surely the crying of the hungry animals reminded the Ninevites that they were humbling themselves before the Lord. Even the livestock in this wicked city were suffering!

> *But let man and beast be covered with*
> *sackcloth, and cry mightily unto God, yea,*
> *let them turn everyone from his evil way, and*
> *from the violence that is in their hands.*
> **Jonah 3:8**

Nothing effects change like strong leadership, and the king of Nineveh caused God's word to be proclaimed and published. Why do churches have leadership seminars? Because leaders affect others, and they must have the right focus in order to direct those who look up to them. Christian leaders should desire to keep the focus on Jesus as we encourage one another in the things of the Lord. Leaders need fellowship and encouragement just as much as others because they must then lead and encourage us.

A strong Christian leader could cause great changes for America today. Billy Graham has said this many times: "If God does not judge the United States, then he is going to have to apologize for Sodom and Gomorrah." God will always judge the wicked and the unrepentant and bring them to their knees. In verse eight, we see that they "*[cried] mightily,*" which implies that this was a matter of great urgency, even life or death. Remember **Jonah 2:7**.

> *"When my soul fainted within me I remembered the LORD: and my prayer came in unto thee, into thine holy temple."*

Jonah remembered Solomon's words and how the Lord promised to hear the prayers of those who cried out for forgiveness. Solomon's prayer, recorded in **II Chronicles 6:32-33**, is a prayer for Gentiles and unbelievers who cry out to the Lord:

> *Moreover concerning the stranger, which is not of thy people Israel, but is come from a far country for thy great name's sake, and thy mighty hand, and thy stretched out arm; if they come and pray in this house; Then hear thou from the heavens, even from thy dwelling place, and do according to all that the stranger calleth to thee for; that all people of the earth may know thy name, and fear thee, as doth thy people Israel, and may know that this house which I have built is called by thy name.*

The sailors on Jonah's ship did not want to perish and neither did the Ninevites! **John 3:15** simply says this,

> *"That whosoever believes in Jesus, should not perish but have everlasting life."*

God does not desire that any people should perish. He wants

them to come to repentance. When you get down to it, no one truly wants to perish for all eternity. These pagan Assyrians fasted and came before the Lord with humility, clothed in sackcloth and ashes. God recognized their sincerity, but they still didn't know what would happen to them.

> *"Who can tell if God will turn and repent,*
> *and turn away from his fierce anger, that we*
> *perish not?"*   **Jonah 3:9**

Did any of us really know what it meant to say that prayer, asking Jesus into our hearts? Of course we didn't fully understand what it meant to be saved or to have eternal life, but we did it because we didn't want to perish. The Ninevites were in the same position. They repented and hoped for deliverance. Why did they think this way? Although he certainly preached judgment, Jonah also shared God's great love and mercy as he speaks of later in chapter four verse two. He could say, with all assurance, that if they called on the name of the Lord, He would hear and save them. Finally, we come to the last verse of Jonah chapter three.

> *And God saw their works, that they turned*
> *from their evil way; and God repented of the*
> *evil, that he had said that he would do unto*
> *them; and he did it not.*   **Jonah 3:10**

This verse says that God repented and He altered his plan. Often we think of the word repent as turning from wrongdoing. Of course, we know that God is incapable of sin, so what does this word mean? The Hebrew word actually means that God made a different decision. He relented, and chose not to destroy Nineveh.

Reading **Jeremiah 18:1-6** will give us another great perspective on God's response to Nineveh's repentance. We read here that God commands Jeremiah to visit the potter's house. Jeremiah observes the potter, who is creating a bowl; however, when the clay gets messed up, the potter refashions it into a beautiful vessel. God Himself is the Potter, and we are the clay. We were all marred with sin, yet He makes us new vessels, doesn't He? Though we were destined for eternal death, God gives us salvation because of our response to Him.

Further on in **Jeremiah 18:8-10** we find two verses that perfectly describe God's decision regarding Nineveh.

> *If that nation, against whom I have pronounced, turn from their evil, I will repent of the evil that I thought to do unto them. And at what instant I shall speak concerning a nation, and concerning a kingdom, to build and to plant it; If it do evil in my sight, that it not obey my voice, then I will repent of the good, wherewith I said I would benefit them.*

God says that He will extend mercy to the nation that repents; however, if this same nation does not heed God's warning, then judgment will come. Whether as an individual or as a nation, our response determines whether we receive blessings or curses from the Lord. I love Paul's words in **Acts 20:21.** He says,

> *"Testifying both to the Jews and also to the Greeks, repentance toward God and faith toward our Lord Jesus Christ."*

Repentance and faith—the Ninevites had both.

In **I Kings 18:21**, Elijah confronts Ahab about the people worshipping Baal. In frustration he asks, *"How long will you halt between two opinions?"* You see, there are two choices here: the Israelites could serve Baal, or they could serve the Lord. We cannot serve two masters. We must make a choice. Jesus, in **Matthew 12:41,** used the Ninevites as an example again:

> *The men of Nineveh shall rise in judgment with this generation, and shall condemn it: because they repented at the preaching of Jonas; and, behold, a greater than Jonas is here.*

Jesus condemned the scribes and Pharisee because they demanded a sign from Him, the very own Son of God; yet the Ninevites immediately responded to Jonah's preaching. In chapter four, we will look at what happens when the Ninevites repent and how that affects Jonah. He reveals his true heart in an interesting way.

Finally, Jonah is running with God. He has received God's message and is on board with God's plan. We cannot run with God until we are open to receiving His word. Once we receive it, God allows an amazing thing to happen. Out of this earthen vessel comes a precious treasure that God commands us to give away. That is why our testimony is so powerful. We share it in order that people might taste and see that the Lord is good. We share God's Word that others might experience the free gift of God—eternal salvation.

STUDY NOTES

STUDY NOTES

CHAPTER 4

RUNNING AHEAD OF GOD

God has saved Nineveh! What a great ending to the book of Jonah. He accomplished his mission for the Lord and as a result, an incredible revival took place in the city. Though the parable of the prodigal son ends with his repentance, God does not stop after Nineveh's salvation. He still has a few lessons to teach Jonah. As we enter the final scene of this book, Jonah's human nature manifests itself, and God pursues and corrects him.

Remember that God is the star, and Jonah is the costar. As we study this book, we need to hone in on the relationship between God and Jonah. As He proves with Jonah, God is always faithful with us. I, for one, am glad that He keeps us in line! God works in us and does not leave us to learn on our own. He is a good Father who chastens His children when they need it.

So far we have seen Jonah running in a variety of directions. He runs *from* God in chapter one, rebelling against God's command. No man can run from God, and Jonah finds this out in a powerful way. Chapter two finds Jonah falling to his knees and running *back* to God. God prepares the fish to save Jonah, who prays for pardon and receives it. In chapter three, Jonah runs *with* God as he preaches in Nineveh. All the people in Nineveh repent, and the Lord saves them. Now, in the final chapter, we will see how Jonah runs *ahead* of God. He begins to question God's mercy and motives.

This is a fascinating study of the human condition. In spite of everything Jonah has experienced, he still has a problem. Jonah needs spiritual heart surgery because of his own selfish attitude.

> *"But it displeased Jonah exceedingly, and he was very angry."*   **Jonah 4:1**

The first verse of chapter four is perplexing. Jonah was not just displeased; he was *extremely* displeased. In other words, Jonah was just plain furious. Imagine that you just witnessed the greatest revival of all time, and pretend that the Lord used you, of all people, to usher in this revival. I know I would feel ecstatic if 600,000 people gave their hearts to Christ because the Lord used me. Jonah didn't, though.

Jonah didn't want these people to receive salvation; instead, he wanted the Ninevites annihilated. He certainly did not want God to show mercy on them. He wanted revenge for all the atrocities the Assyrians had committed. However, the real problem here lies with Jonah, not with the people of Nineveh. As we will see, God has a plan to deal with Jonah.

> *And he prayed unto the LORD, and said, I pray thee, O LORD, was not this my saying, when I was yet in my country? Therefore I fled before unto Tarshish: for I knew that thou art a gracious God, and merciful, slow to anger, and of great kindness, and repentest thee of the evil. Therefore now, O LORD, take, I beseech thee, my life from me; for it is better for me to die than to live.*   **Jonah 4:2-3**

Jonah has two prayers recorded in this book. We find the first one in chapter two when Jonah is in the belly of the fish. His heart was broken before the Lord, and he cried out in his affliction. It was an honest, desperate plea. Jonah's worst situation brought about his best prayer.

In contrast, Jonah now finds himself in an ideal situation. He is in Nineveh, and God is working through him to bring everyone to repentance. This should be a time of rejoicing, but instead Jonah offers up his worst prayer. He is insensitive and hardhearted. His first prayer was, "Lord, save me," and now he is praying, "Lord, kill me." Jonah would rather die than see the Lord save the Ninevites. Jonah's prayer in verse three reveals his heart.

Initially, Jonah did not run from God out of fear. He ran because he knew that God loves everyone. He knew God would save the Ninevites if they repented. He may have said to himself, "If I go to the Ninevites, they will probably get saved. God is so loving and full of kindness. He is willing to forgive anyone. I don't want any part of that!" As we have seen previously, Jonah had no love for the Ninevites.

Thankfully, God never changes. His attributes remain the same yesterday, today, and tomorrow. Some people read the Old Testament and see God as full of wrath, destroying everyone who gets in His way. Notice, though, that God is gracious to the Ninevites. He is compassionate, slow to anger, and abounding in love. It is Jonah who is full of wrath.

There is an interesting exchange between Abraham and God in **Genesis 18**. God was planning on destroying Sodom and Gomorrah because of their great sins. Abraham did not understand God's plan, and he questioned it. **Genesis 18:23** says,

> *"And Abraham drew near, and said, Wilt thou also destroy the righteous with the wicked?"*

Abraham began to barter with the Lord, asking him to spare Sodom and Gomorrah on account of fifty righteous people. God said He would spare the fifty, and Abraham then asked if God would spare the city on account of forty righteous men. He continued bartering until God agreed to withhold His wrath for the sake of only ten righteous men. As it turned out, only eight righteous people could be found. Though God destroyed the city, he spared these eight because He is righteous and compassionate.

Horace Bushnell once said that forgiveness is both man's deepest need and his highest achievement. Jonah's anger stemmed from the fact that he knew God would forgive the Ninevites. For a child of God, his attitude was wrong. We need to love our brothers and sisters in the Lord, no matter what they are like. When we belong to the Lord, He changes our hearts and lives and shows us how to forgive. **Ephesians 4:32** says,

> *"And be ye kind one to another, tenderhearted, forgiving one another, even as God for Christ's sake hath forgiven you."*

Think about this verse for a minute. God has forgiven all of the sins we have ever committed. Are we then going to be angry with somebody else? Are we going to try to take revenge on another person or hold a grudge against them? Is that what it means to live for Christ? No! We need to put off the old man, and put on the mind of Christ.

Jonah only cared about his own reputation. He was worried people would brand him a false prophet once they found out the Ninevites were spared. Here was Jonah, prophesying doom and gloom, but instead the Ninevites repented and were spared. Jonah also feared what his Jewish brothers would say once they found out his role in Nineveh's deliverance.

To Jonah, the Ninevites were just fodder for the fires of hell; but in God's eyes, the Ninevites were repentant sinners. God desired their salvation. Can you imagine the rejoicing in heaven over 600,000 saved souls? Jonah could not handle it. He was more worried about his reputation than his character. How many times have we found this type of thinking in history? In our own lives?

Jonah's character was being tested. Instead of trusting the Lord, he was ready to die. He lacked faith. Another Old Testament prophet experienced a similar lapse. His name was Elijah. Queen Jezebel, the evil wife of King Ahab, put a contract out on Elijah's life, and he was running away from her as fast as he could. This happened right after he had a great victory in the Lord. God used Elijah to wipe out 450 prophets of the false god Baal. But Elijah found himself burned out physically, emotionally, and spiritually. Jonah is in a similar state. He was angry and exhausted, and he desired death.

> *"Then said the LORD, Doest thou well to be*
> *angry?"*   **Jonah 4:4**

God asks Jonah, "Is doing good displeasing to you?" We

know that God is in the business of salvation. When even one sinner repents, all of heaven celebrates! Jonah does not celebrate, though, and his anger is completely unfounded. Vengeance belongs to the Lord, not to Jonah, and not to us. Jonah was so full of anger that he wanted death! Intense anger can cause sickness of all kinds within us. When you struggle with anger, ask the Lord to give you peace.

> *So Jonah went out of the city, and sat on the east side of the city, and there made him a booth, and sat under it in the shadow, till he might see what would become of the city.*
> **Jonah 4:5**

Jonah starts running again, but this time he runs ahead of God. He goes outside the city and finds a perch where he can watch God's proceedings with Nineveh. He has a front row seat, so he takes a little time to build a hooded cover for shade.

Jonah should have stayed in the city, but once again, he strays from God's command. When you wander from God's calling on your life, you are almost guaranteed depression. Here, we find another similarity between Jonah and the parable of the prodigal son. In the story, the prodigal's older brother is furious because he resents the younger son's warm homecoming after all the hurt he had caused. When the father threw a feast for his long lost son, the older brother would not join in. **Luke 15:28** tells us,

> *"And he was angry, and would not go in: therefore came his father out, and intreated him."*

Instead of being happy that his brother was safe, he pouted and allowed his anger to take hold, just like Jonah did.

Jonah could have continued to bless the people in Nineveh, but he was too stubborn. He preferred to sit and wallow in self-pity, but Jonah kept watch in case God would destroy the city after all. Clearly, Jonah did not think they had a true conversion, and he waited for God to rain fire and brimstone on them.

Have you ever felt that way about someone? Have you ever criticized a person going forward to receive Christ? Perhaps you thought to yourself, "Yeah, right, go forward, but it isn't going to take." Maybe somebody you know has professed faith but always seems to fail in his or her walk. Instead of being excited for that person, you act cynical and self-righteous. Now Jonah finds himself in this place spiritually.

We can picture Jonah up there, sitting and waiting under the little booth he made for himself. Jonah tried to make his own shade. He wanted to shield himself from the hot sun. We need to be careful about trying to make it on our own. When we try to accomplish things on our own, pride creeps in. Jonah probably looked at the booth he made and said, "Look at that! I did a great job." Then he sat under it and realized it was still hot and miserable. We cannot imagine what God will do for Jonah next. I know if I were in charge, I'd want to blast Jonah a few times for his attitude! However, God blesses Jonah.

> *And the LORD God prepared a gourd, and made it to come up over Jonah, that it might be a shadow over his head, to deliver him from his grief. So Jonah was exceeding glad of the gourd.*   **Jonah 4:6**

God showed His kindness by causing a gourd to grow over Jonah and protect him from the sun. God replaced Jonah's work with His own. What exactly was this gourd? We aren't sure what type of plant this was, but many believe it was some kind of palm that grew rapidly. In two or three days, it grew several feet and produced huge leaves for shade. God decided to bless Jonah, even though Jonah's attitude was sinful.

There are times in our lives when we rebel. We lack fellowship with the Lord, and our prayer life dwindles. During these times, God will sometimes bless us. Why does God do this? Certainly not because we deserve it! God blesses us because His goodness brings us to repentance. Even when we show disobedience and anger, God puts a shade over us.

Jonah experiences God's grace, which by definition is unmerited favor. We may look at Jonah and think, "But he shouldn't receive God's grace with that attitude!" Maybe the most important question is this: do any of us deserve God's grace? Look at how we act. Each and every one of us sins continually, yet God forgives us. We should treat our brothers and sisters the same way.

I heard a story once about a church secretary. She received a call from a man who asked to speak to the "Chief Hog of the Trough." This struck her as odd, so she inquired further,

"Who did you want to speak to?"

The man repeated, "The Chief Hog of the Trough."

The secretary answered, "Sir, are you talking about our pastor? You should have a little more respect. This is a church you are calling."

The man then said, "Oh, I'm sorry. I just called because I wanted to donate $100,000 to the church building fund."

At that, the secretary quickly said, "I think I see that hog coming down the hallway right now." Sometimes we think more of ourselves than we should. God's grace reminds us of who we are and who He is. It is true that our nature has changed since we received Christ, but look at what we were before Christ. After giving our hearts to Jesus, we can identify with what Paul said in **Romans 7:18**.

> *For I know that in me (that is, in my flesh,) dwelleth no good thing: for to will is present with me; but how to perform that which is good I find not.*

We sometimes fall off-track and find ourselves in sin. There is nothing inherently good in us, except that which is done by Christ. Even when we sin, God is still faithful, and He blesses us.

An interesting thing about Jonah here is that he was grieving. We have to wonder, was Jonah grieving because of the heat of the day? Surely that was part of it. But I think that most of Jonah's grief stemmed from his great anger. Anger always causes grief. As soon as God blessed Jonah, he became exceedingly glad, but look what happened right after that.

> *But God prepared a worm when the morning*
> *rose the next day, and it smote the gourd that*
> *it withered.*   **Jonah 4:7**

God provided the gourd to shade Jonah, and then He provided something else: a worm to kill the gourd. What exactly is God doing here? First, He blessed Jonah by providing shade, and then He took that comfort away. Sometimes bad things do come from the Lord, but He allows them in order to help us mature. But for Jonah, this trial seemed like the last straw.

All of us deal with worms from time to time. Problems can be worms, just gnawing away at your life. Have you ever noticed how worms always seem to come along just when we have become attached to something? God sends worms our way to get our attention because He loves us. He wants us to see what is truly important. Where are our priorities?

We all know the story of the Titanic. In April of 1912, this great ship hit an iceberg and sank on its maiden voyage. As the ship went down, a woman on board ran downstairs instead of toward the lifeboats. To some, it seemed that she was running to collect valuables—gold or silver she had left behind. Instead, she returned with some oranges from her stateroom. She did not care about her earthly riches. She knew she could live longer in the lifeboat with the oranges. In a life and death predicament, our priorities change.

When God allows worms to remove something important, we have a chance to refocus and get back to basics. In **Matthew 6:33**, Jesus said,

> *"But seek ye first the kingdom of God, and his righteousness; and all these things shall be added unto you."*

1 Thessalonians 5:18 says,

> *"In everything give thanks; for this is the will of God in Christ Jesus concerning you."*

This means to give thanks in your blessings and in your trials. In everything, no matter what you are going through, give thanks. Job was a man who had it all and lost it all. Despite his trial, he continued to love the Lord. He made an amazing statement in **Job 1:21**,

> *"The LORD gave, and the LORD hath taken away; blessed be the name of the LORD."*

Job endured more grief and loss than most of us can imagine, yet his love for the Lord remained unwavering. We can only be like Job if we keep our eyes on the Lord.

In **2 Samuel 16** King David fled when his son Absalom seized power. A relative of King Saul, Shimei, began to curse and taunt David. He was David's little worm. Shimei began calling David names and eventually began to throw stones at David and his entourage. Finally, one of David's soldiers, Abishai, offered to kill Shimei. David's response was amazing. He simply told Abishai to leave Shimei alone and let him curse. David made an important realization. He recognized that the Lord had allowed this worm into his life. Rather than letting his emotions rule his actions, David relied on his spiritual discernment.

In contrast, Jonah seems to lack any spiritual discernment, and God is still dealing with him. First God blessed Jonah, and then He took that blessing away. But God still has a way of getting Jonah's attention.

> *And it came to pass, when the sun did arise, that God prepared a vehement east wind; and the sun beat upon the head of Jonah, that he fainted, and wished in himself to die, and said, It is better for me to die than to live.*
> **Jonah 4:8**

So far we have seen God give Jonah a gourd to provide him shade and a worm to take the shade away. God now causes the unbearably hot east wind to blow on Jonah. God is working to repair Jonah's heart. The east wind represents trials we all face in life.

In **Matthew 7:24-27**, Jesus spoke about these winds. He told a parable of two men. One of them built his house on a rock and one built his house on the sand. When the winds and storms came, the house on the rock stood firm. Why did it stand? Because this house was built on the strong foundation of Christ. When the trials of life struck the house on the sand, it fell flat. It could not survive on such an unstable foundation.

We tend to see the storms of life in a completely negative light, but we must reform our thinking. These storms help us in two major ways. First, they cause us to look back and appreciate yesterday's weather. We can say, "Wow, I don't like what I am going through today, but thank God for yesterday." Second, they help us look forward to what God will accomplish through the storm. We must have a sure foundation in Christ to endure these trials with understanding rather than anger.

Another reason God called up the east wind is to get Jonah to move! Right now, he is sitting outside the city pouting, but God wants him inside the city, rejoicing with the Ninevites. Jonah should be thanking God for saving these people; instead, he sulks at the point of suicide. God patiently tries to move him along to a better location.

Jonah's isolation gave him the blues. If you isolate yourself by pulling out of fellowship with the Lord and other believers, you will suffer. Our happiness comes from being right with Christ, and we cannot have that without fellowship. How do you get rid of the blues? The following list will help us overcome our spiritual depression.

1. Do something good for somebody else
2. Do something good for somebody else
3. Do something good for somebody else
4. Do something good for somebody else
5. Do something good for somebody else
6. Do something good for somebody else
7. Do something good for somebody else

8. Do something good for somebody else
9. Do something good for somebody else
10. Do something good for somebody else

Serving others is our key to getting out of a slump. Your depression will melt away when you willingly give yourself to helping others. Are you feeling a strong wind against you today? Maybe God is trying to help you refocus. Right now is a good time to help somebody else.

1 Peter 4:12-13 says:

> *Beloved, think it not strange concerning the fiery trial which is to try you, as though some strange thing happened unto you: But rejoice, inasmuch as ye are partakers of Christ's sufferings; that, when his glory shall be revealed, ye may be glad also with exceeding joy.*

God sends these winds to improve our heart and find out where our faith lies. Trials are a part of the Christian life, and they reveal our true hearts. Yes, they can be unpleasant, but God uses them to help us mature.

The Gourd, the Worm, and the Wind

God used the process of the gourd, the worm, and the wind to get Jonah's attention. The gourd was God's blessing on Jonah. The worm was Jonah's trial and the removal of the blessing. With the east wind, God prompted Jonah to move. The Lord allowed all three experiences for the purpose of repairing Jonah. He needed an eternal perspective, rather than merely looking for creature comforts. He was not seeing things from God's point of view.

When the heat began to rise, Jonah must have thought back to the belly of the fish. God reminded him what it feels like to be lost. Being lost is miserable. Jonah needed reminding because of his materialistic focus. He certainly was unstable! One minute he is preaching God's salvation and the next he is hopeless and pitiful. Jonah cries out for rescue from the fish, but once he is rescued, he asks God to let him die! Jonah was double-minded and his heart was in the wrong place.

Ironically, Jonah seems to be the only one in this book who disobeys God. The Ninevites repent and obey. The great fish obeys. Even the gourd, the worm, and the wind obey God. Not Jonah, though. He continues to dig in his heels, and he cares more about his own comfort than saving lost souls.

This begs an interesting question: do you have to love people to bring them the gospel? Do you have to love a certain country in order to be a missionary? It certainly helps! But as we see in Jonah, the surprising answer is no. Jonah hated the Ninevites. Yes, he preached and they repented, but Jonah certainly felt no love for them. What we must understand, though, is that God loved the Ninevites. He saved them, not Jonah. Jonah was only God's mouthpiece.

Many missionaries have gone to a foreign country only to find that they do not like it. Before they left, they said, "I love those people." Maybe they even went on a few short-term mission trips to the country and felt they had a strong relationship with the people there. Then, when they actually go there long-term, things change. They find themselves in a new place with a different language and different customs. Difficulties adjusting may leave them with no love for the very people they came to minister to. They answered the call God placed on their lives for the people that *He* loves. Sometimes, the missionaries may develop a newfound love for the people, but not always. God never places us in vain. Don't be like Jonah and wallow in self-pity. Seek God's face, and He will direct you and change your heart.

> *"And God said to Jonah, Doest thou well to be angry for the gourd? And he said, I do well to be angry, even unto death."*   **Jonah 4:9**

God questions Jonah about his anger. Jonah's creature comforts have been taken away, so he answers the Lord that he deserves to be angry. He even goes so far as to say that he should die. In this situation, God really reveals Jonah's selfishness and bitter heart. Jonah pities the gourd, but he has no love for the people of Nineveh.

Sometimes, instead of caring about the people around us, we put our energies into our plants, our pets, or other hobbies. We treat our creature comforts as if they were people. God teaches Jonah, and us, a heavy lesson here. People are always more important because they have souls that will never die.

Then said the LORD, Thou hast had pity on the
gourd, for the which thou hast not laboured,
neither madest it grow; which came up in a
night, and perished in a night: And should
not I spare Nineveh, that great city, wherein
are more than sixscore thousand persons that
cannot discern between their right hand and
their left hand; and also much cattle?

Jonah 4:10-11

The book of Jonah has an unusual ending. It ends with a question. God asks Jonah, "Should I not spare Nineveh, that great city, where there are at least 120,000 persons who cannot tell their right hand from their left? And so many cattle?" What is the Lord saying here, and why does he mention only 120,000 people?

We know there were at least 600,000 people in Nineveh. Many believe the 120,000 mentioned here are the children of Nineveh. These innocent children were too young to know right from wrong. God also mentions the cattle. He cared about them as well. Even in His final question in this book, God teaches Jonah to have compassion on every creature.

We cannot truly love people until we know them. Jonah did not know the Ninevites, but God uses children to get Jonah's attention. He is saying, "Jonah, can you love children? Can you care about them?" I find it interesting that many television ads use children, especially when it comes to giving. They will show a child who looks malnourished, and our sympathy immediately goes out to them. Children have a way of gripping our hearts because they are defenseless. Who is going to save them?

The Gospel of **Mark 10:13** records a remarkable story about children.

> *"And they brought young children to Him that He should touch them: and His disciples rebuked those that brought them."*

People from everywhere brought their children to Jesus so that He could bless them. Jesus' disciples got upset and rebuked the parents. When Jesus saw His disciples' actions, He was very displeased. Jesus wanted the children to come to Him, and He took the children up in His arms and blessed them. He said in Mark 10:15, "Verily I say unto you, whosoever shall not receive the kingdom of God as a little child, he shall not enter therein." Does God love children? Yes, He loves them very much. Jonah only cared about a gourd that he had no part in planting or raising, yet he had no compassion for the people, not even the children. God wants to replace Jonah's heart of stone with a heart of flesh, and He asks a simple question. "Jonah, shouldn't I have pity on this people? Shouldn't I spare them?" Jonah's answer is not recorded in the Scriptures. We don't need to know Jonah's final answer in order to learn from this book.

If you ever visit Rome and the Sistine Chapel, look for Jonah. Michelangelo painted the faces of the prophets, apostles, and patriarchs all over the ceiling. When you see Jonah's face, you will notice it is the brightest face of all. Jonah glows with excitement, more than the other faces on the ceiling. I read an article about this unusual feature, and the author said, "Maybe Michelangelo knew something we don't." Did

Jonah receive his heart of flesh? Maybe he found the answer to his dilemma in God's question. Maybe God took Jonah's anger and replaced it with His compassion.

Our hope is for Jonah to repent and receive a new heart just as the prodigal son did. We want to see Jonah come to his senses and begin rejoicing with the Ninevites in the city. We want to see him acknowledging God's mercy, loving-kindness, and goodness. We want to see him come to a place where he says simply, "I was lost, and now I am found." The important question, however, is this: how does your story end?

How Does Your Story End?

What do you care most about in this life? What is your number one priority? Do you care for temporal things or eternal things? After Jesus returned to heaven, His apostles had to look to the eternal things to keep them going.

II Corinthians 4:16 says,

> *"For which cause we faint not; but though our outward man perish, yet the inward man is renewed day by day."*

Just as with the apostles and Jonah, God deals with us on a daily basis. He renews our inward man continually and changes our heart to focus on eternity. We may face worms, but in light of eternity, they only last for a fleeting moment. We may not always see God's purpose because we have our eyes on the temporal things. We must look beyond earthly things and realize that our hope lies in eternity.

Are you too focused on the temporal today? Pray for the

Lord to send you a worm. You can pray a simple prayer: "Lord, I am doing something that is taking me away from You. It is sitting on my heart's throne, and it shouldn't be there. You should be there. Lord, please deal with me. If this is not of You, take it from me. Remove it from me." Why is it so important to remove the temporal from our lives and gain an eternal perspective? In **John 14:1-3** Jesus tells us:

> *Let not your heart be troubled: ye believe in God, believe also in me. In my Father's house are many mansions: if it were not so, I would have told you. I go to prepare a place for you. And if I go and prepare a place for you, I will come again, and receive you unto myself; that where I am, there ye may be also.*

God is preparing a place for us, and He is also preparing us for that place. He works constantly on our hearts and minds. Jesus will come back again to take us and He wants us to be ready. Therefore our prayer should be, "Lord, do whatever it takes to prepare me." If God decides to use blessings in our lives, we should rejoice. If He sends worms, and we have a few trials, rejoice as well! We cannot fight His work in our lives.

Matthew 12:41 reminds us that one greater than Jonah has come in Jesus. Jonah's message was judgment, but Jesus' message is grace and salvation. **John 3:16-17** says:

> *For God so loved the world, that he gave his only begotten Son, that whosoever believeth in him should not perish, but have everlasting life. For God sent not his Son into the world to condemn the world; but that the world*

through him might be saved.

God sent His Son to the entire world, not just a city. This is why Jesus commanded His disciples to go into the entire world to make new disciples. Today we need a world vision. We need to see beyond the city and even the country. We need the Lord's vision, which includes the entire world, even those you see as your enemies. Every single person alive needs the Lord. The best prayer we can make for them is this, "Lord, bring them to the end of themselves. Bring them to You." In order to do this, our hearts must be right toward others.

God loves to work with us in this area. He loves to show us His mercy and grace, so that we can impart it to somebody else. Before He can do this, though, we need to ask ourselves two questions. First, do we care about the lost? If we do, then the second question is what are we doing about it? In **Acts 1:8**, Jesus told His disciples:

> *But ye shall receive power, after that the Holy Ghost is come upon you: and ye shall be witnesses unto me both in Jerusalem, and in all Judaea, and in Samaria, and unto the uttermost part of the earth.*

Do we have the power of the Holy Spirit to help us care for those who are lost?

Although we do not have Jonah's answers to these questions, we do know our own personal answers. Have we called upon the Lord to guide us? Do we know that He is the God of second chances? At one time or another, we have all blown it. We all make mistakes, but the Lord forgives us. When we call upon Him, He dusts us off and sends us out again. Do we have a repentant attitude? Are we ready for the work of the Lord?

Your attitude is so important because many times it is your only witness. When you are a Christian, people watch you and will pick up on your attitude immediately. Where your heart is, there is your treasure. If we seek the Kingdom of God first, everything else will be taken care of. Jesus wants us to be His representatives to the world, and He will do whatever it takes to get us there.

Mark 16:20 tells us,

> *"And they went forth, and preached everywhere, the Lord working with them, and confirming the word with signs following."*

With our attitude and focus on the Lord, He enables us. When the Lord sends us, He is the One working in us, with us, and through us. Without the Lord, we cannot effectually accomplish His work. When He is with us, He gives us signs to confirm the work we do for Him. People will come to know Him. Lives will be changed. God will use us to plant and water seeds, and the Lord will give increase. People around us will know God's incredible forgiveness, just as the Ninevites did.

Conclusion

The Book of Jonah begins with God's calling and ends with God's question to the prophet Jonah. God is the star of the book. Jonah has spent a lot of time running from

Him, running to Him, running with Him, and finally running ahead of Him. Through it all, God has not let Jonah go. God began the work in Jonah, and even though we did not hear the end of his story, we have confidence that God finished it. In the same manner, God has begun a work in you, and He will be faithful to complete it. He will never leave you or forsake you.

Have you been fighting God's will in your life? If you want to receive His forgiveness right now, you can. The price for our sins was enormous. Jesus died on the cross to remove them, but he makes it so easy to receive Him. Take the time right now to bow your head. Honestly and openly ask the Lord to forgive you. Admit to Him what you have been hiding; He already knows your secrets anyway. Ask Him into your life. Begin to read your Bible and pray to God every day. Join a Bible teaching fellowship, and share your testimony. Then buckle your seatbelt. God has an amazing plan for you, just as He did for Jonah.

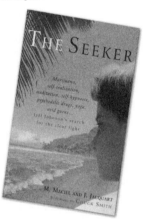

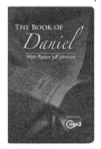

STUDY NOTES

STUDY NOTES